"THAT'S NOT RIGHT!"

My life living with
Asperger's

"THAT'S NOT RIGHT!"

My life living with
Asperger's

To callie

Manners

Alex Manners

CAVALCADE BOOKS

First published in the United Kingdom in 2019

by Cavalcade Books
www.cavalcadebooks.com

ISBN 978-1-9996213-5-3

Cover photography by Stephen Manners
Cover design by Colourburst Lithographic Ltd

"That's not right!" I shouted as I walked up the hill (well, slight slope) on the way to school. I then said, "I'm writing to Tony Blair. Why has he not made all the roads flat?"

You see, the world around me was confusing and many things did not seem right to me.

CONTENTS

PREFACE

The biggest challenge that I have faced in my life living with Asperger's is school. When I wasn't at school I was dreading going to school. When I was at school I felt as though I was in prison and I had a terrible time.

A few years ago, I asked my dad if he had any information about my Asperger's to include in a piece I had been writing about my Asperger's and my love of football. I was shocked when he handed me two enormous boxes containing file after file of notes on discussions, meetings and communications from my initial diagnosis of Asperger's to when I finally left sixth form. My dad's "notes" were the inspiration for me to write an article about my life living with Asperger's. I then wrote other articles, was interviewed on radio and TV, and then wrote this book.

This book documents my life growing up with Asperger's, both at home and at school, in the hope that it will help other people like me and especially raise awareness of problems at school for children with Asperger's.

FOREWORD

As Alex's father, it was a relief to get a diagnosis of Asperger's for him. For his mother and me, it meant that we could educate ourselves about Asperger's and hopefully by doing so understand him better and consequently be more able to help him.

The process for getting Alex diagnosed was a long and arduous one, especially as everything about Asperger's was alien to us. Once diagnosed and with a Statement of Special Educational Needs, we naïvely thought things would improve. In many respects they did, but it was still a case of having to fight for everything Alex needed. The ignorance and incompetence that we faced were overwhelming at times. Dealing with schools and the Local Education Authority was frustrating and very time consuming. My real concern on this journey has always been that, whilst I am capable of being able to fight the system, most parents are not. So, what happens to their children? A lot needs to be altered at a governmental level in order to properly address the needs of children with Asperger's.

Along the way, we were lucky enough to get advice and help from some exceptional people who were instrumental in helping us get Alex the support he required. Such people as David Wort, the founder of Family Equip, the SENCO (Special Educational Needs Co-ordinator) and Alex's personal assistant at Alex's secondary school, and the child psychiatrist from CAMHS (Child and Adolescent Mental Health Services), to name a few.

Seeing Alex grow up with all the anxiety and stress that he did was extremely difficult. It had a huge impact on the whole family too. However, it is wonderful to see how he has used his positive, determined "never give up" attitude to become the person he is today. Without any prompting, he has given his time to help other children with Asperger's at the charity Family Equip, he has raised money via various means for that charity, he has set up his own business doing video production, he has his own children's radio show, even written his own children's story called "Rainbow Man", appeared on live TV, he now does talks at national Asperger's events, presents to schools, universities and businesses about his life living with Asperger's, and the list goes on. He is a unique, quirky and loveable character, who from a difficult start in life has transformed himself into a happy and fulfilled person pursuing his passions. We're all very proud of you, Alex!

Andrew Manners

WHAT IS ASPERGER'S?

For me, the most important thing about autism and Asperger's to note is that everyone is different. As autism expert Dr Stephen Shore said, "Once you have met one person with autism, you have met one person with autism!"

Asperger's is a form of autism on the autistic spectrum. It affects how we communicate with others and how we make sense of the world around us. Everyone with Asperger's is unique, like a piece of a jigsaw. We can struggle to process language, have a love of routine, are prone to sensory issues and we usually have a subject that we are obsessed with. We can also struggle to read facial expressions, jokes and common phrases.

That was my definition of Asperger's; however, the National Autistic Society have provided a more detailed description, which can be found at the end of the book.

ABOUT ME

My name is Alex Manners, I am twenty-two and I have Asperger's, a form of autism. I was diagnosed with Asperger's when I was ten, back in 2007, and although I look upon my Asperger's as a positive, there were many challenges that I had to face, especially whilst at school. Another thing that you should know about me is that I am obsessed with football and I am trying to visit all 92 Football League grounds to see a match at each one with my Uncle Tim. I have done 89 so far (February 2019).

From an early age, my parents recall me often saying, "That's not right!" With hindsight, they believe this was the first sign of my Asperger's. I guess the world around me seemed very confusing and nothing seemed to make sense.

From the age of four, I attended my local primary school. I did not enjoy my time there and was often bullied, not only by some of my classmates but also, in my opinion, by some of the teachers. I always felt that the teachers there failed to understand my Asperger's and as a consequence did not treat me in the right way.

At the age of eleven, I moved to a private secondary school, 9 miles away, where I stayed until I completed my A-Levels in the sixth form. I enjoyed my first three years at secondary school much more than I had enjoyed my time at primary school. I had a smaller class size, teachers who understood me better and friends who also had Asperger's, who I felt that I could relate to. The school also had a wonderful SENCO who really understood me and helped me enormously (such as allowing me to not have to do homework, which was a major issue for me).

However, after three years, a new headteacher arrived at the school and, for me, things started to change for the worse. The years when I was doing my GCSEs were the most traumatic years I had at the school. This was because many changes were introduced, undoing some of the good things that had been put in place for people with Asperger's. My stress levels rose at this point and I started to feel more uncomfortable at school. I felt that some individuals within the school were failing to understand my Asperger's and sometimes failing to even acknowledge the existence of it! My dad, concerned about the deterioration of my mental health, contacted the school to discuss my issues with all the changes. But the only result of this was that my dad was banned from attending any meetings at the school!

My dad contacted the council but failed to get any help from them. I was unaware of this at the time, but it became apparent that the real problem was that, as the school was an independent school, it did not fall under the jurisdiction of the Local Education Authority.

At this time, in order to help me cope with the enormous stress I was under, I was referred back to the NHS.

As soon as I started in the sixth form, I felt a lot happier and a lot more relaxed. This was because some of the things that my dad had argued that I needed right from when I first started the school, such as wearing my own clothes and having more free time, were put in place.

I have a number of ambitions (you can find a list of these at the end of the book), but my main one is to become a TV presenter. I currently present my own radio show and run my own business creating promotional videos for companies and sports clubs. As well as this, I also present talks on "My Life Living with Asperger's". I am determined to live my life doing the things I enjoy and "pursuing my passions", and I will never give up until my ambitions are achieved.

CHAPTER 1
Being diagnosed with Asperger's

"According to Department for Education figures, there was a 35% increase between 2015 and 2016 in the number of local authority refusals to carry out EHC [Education, Health and Care] needs assessments on children. And for those who did get an assessment, in just over 40% of cases, the family had to wait longer than the 20 weeks cut-off date by which a decision whether to approve an EHC plan should be made, as councils struggle to do their job with the funding they have."

The Guardian, Tuesday, 5th September 2017

I was born in Solihull on 4th November 1996. Up until the age of one, I used to go to the hospital or have a home visit from the doctor about two or three times a month. Then from the age of one until I was about three, I still used to go to the hospital or have a home visit regularly but not quite so often, about once a month. These visits were mainly to see how I was feeding and eating and how I was generally progressing in weight, height etc. I also had to have a lot of different tests, including one on my heart and one for cystic fibrosis. It was also around this time that I was referred to an orthopaedic surgeon about my feet and went to Solihull Hospital to see a paediatrician.

From a very young age, I have always been a little bit different, even though at the time I did not know it. When I was born, I was classified as being in the "0 percentile", which meant that I was not developing at the normal rate. This was because I was "failing to thrive". The doctors were not worried as this most often corrects itself, and they even prescribed me something to help build up my weight. As a young lad, I had what was known as "hypermobile joints", meaning that I could extend my joints beyond the normal range of motion. This meant that I didn't walk until I was two. To try and combat this, I had to wear "Pedro boots" and have special insoles made (called orthotics), something that I still wear in my shoes today. I also had a few operations, including an operation in July 2001 at the Birmingham Children's Hospital to remove a squint that I had in one eye, and another operation to insert grommets into my ears. As you can tell, I had to go to the doctors quite often. From the age of two, I have also worn glasses. However, my sight is getting better and recently my optician said that in a few years' time I may no longer need to wear glasses.

Before I got to the age of seven, I would not really eat many things. In fact, one of the only things that I would eat was butter. To try and get me to gain weight and to try other foods, my grandad used to feed cream to me from a syringe. However, once I hit the age of seven, I started to become a very good eater and would eat foods that most children of that age would not even touch. I remember going to a fish restaurant with my grandparents, and when I ordered mussels, they told me that I could not have them because they did not think I would know how to eat them. I told them that I did know how to eat them as I had had them before and they were quite shocked that I not only knew this but that I actually liked them. By this time, I had caught up with my ideal weight and was even a little bit chubby.

Writing lists was something that I did a lot of. I used to write lists on every topic imaginable from family members to parts of the body and favourite songs. It used to be a way for me to have some order and control in my life. It was also very therapeutic and relaxing. When I was looking through all of my dad's notes, I found a magazine that I had made when I was younger called "Alex Special". Inside it contained jokes, recipes, things that I do and things about me. It also included lots of lists on food and drink, animals, parts of the body and my school friends.

The first time that anybody thought that I may have Asperger's was when we were on holiday in America. We were staying with family friends in Florida and one of them noticed that I became stressed very easily. His son had Asperger's and he thought that I may have it as well. He gave my nan a book on Asperger's, who later passed it on to my parents. That was the first time my parents had ever heard of Asperger's.

In November 2005, I was referred to the Meadow Centre by the SENCO at my primary school. Then in January 2006, I was put on a waiting list to be assessed for Asperger's. They told us that this could be a lengthy process and that for some people it can take up to three years to be diagnosed. However, it only took a year for me to be diagnosed. Two months after being referred to the Meadow Centre, my mum rang them up to see if the whole process could be speeded up and said that she would be willing to come in at short notice if there were any cancellations. It was a further two months before I was top of the waiting list for assessment.

My first appointment at the Meadow Centre was in July 2006 with a consultant Clinical Psychologist and a Speech and Language Therapist. The appointment was more of an "informal session" where they played a variety of games with me and I told them what I found easy and difficult. They gave me a photocopy of the notes they had taken of the answers I had given to keep, as well as a "Children's Communication Checklist" to complete and bring back next time. It said things such as, "Does he talk repetitively about things that no one is interested in?" and "fails to recognise when people are upset or angry?" After that first appointment, I wanted to go back. I did not know why I had to go to the Meadow Centre, but all the attention I was getting as well as the fact that they had told me that I had a high IQ made me feel special.

On another trip to the Meadow Centre, in November 2006, I had a "cognitive assessment" by an Assistant Clinical Psychologist. I was asked a number of different questions. These included "picture concepts" where I had to choose two pictures that went together e.g. *bat* and *ball*, "meanings" where I had to say what certain words meant e.g. migrate, and "digit span" where I had to repeat patterns of numbers backwards. I was given a few items that I had to make up a story about. I told a story about a car on an obstacle course. They also asked questions such as, "Do you do anything annoying?", "What are you afraid of?" and "Do you have friends?"

I was finally diagnosed with Asperger's Syndrome in January 2007 when I was ten years old. I was sitting in a room at my primary school in a meeting with my parents and the school SENCO. The SENCO suddenly said to me, "By the way Alex, do you realise you have Asperger's?" I had no idea what this was at the time or what it meant. I just sat there and nodded. To be honest, I felt a tad confused. When I came out of the room my dad told me that I should not be worried about having Asperger's because many of our family members have Asperger's traits and that it gives us special powers e.g. being creative and thinking differently. I believed him and so from then on, I have always viewed my Asperger's as something positive and something that I feel lucky to have. Although I look upon my Asperger's as a positive, there were many challenges that I had to face, especially whilst at school.

Many teachers did not understand my Asperger's, especially at my primary school, and I feel some did not want to take any notice of it. They wanted to treat me exactly the same as everyone else, which is something that you can't do with an autistic individual. Only after receiving my Statement of Special Educational Needs in 2007 did things change. However, in order for the teachers to take any notice of my Statement, my dad had to arrange for an emergency meeting at the school where someone from the council came in. They made it clear to the teachers that they were legally obliged to follow the instructions in the Statement and to treat me accordingly. A few things were put in place, such as the "time outs" I was allowed to have if I was feeling stressed, but for me not a lot changed.

A little knowledge is a dangerous thing. Sometimes when a person knows a little bit about something, they feel like they're an expert. Because they feel like an expert, they try to do things that they shouldn't and they can mess things up.

CHAPTER 2
Primary school

"63% of children on the autism spectrum are not in the kind of school their parents believe would best support them."

The National Autistic Society, Autism facts and history

At my primary school I did not feel accepted at all and hated my time there. I felt like I was in prison and that all of the teachers were like prison officers, forcing us to do things, treating us exactly the same as how prisoners would be treated in prison. I had one particular friend at the school who was diagnosed with Asperger's a few years after me. We both felt isolated and as though everyone hated us.

In Year 4 my problems at school started to get worse. One incident that I remember vividly involved a piece of homework. During one lesson I was sitting at a table and the teacher asked for our homework. Homework was something that I hated as I could not accept that we had to do work at home. As she got around to collecting mine, I tore it up in front of her and told her that the dog did it, even though I did not have a dog. I just hated homework and was so angry that I had used my own time to complete this homework that tearing it up was my way of showing the teacher how I felt. All she ended up doing was making me tape my homework back together and moved me on to the next table.

A lot of the time in primary school I would get into such a state over my homework that my mum would do it for me. On the occasions when I did it myself I would deliberately do it badly. The writing would be really messy with some small and some big letters as my attitude was well at least I have done something. As I saw it, school was for work and home was for play. I couldn't come to terms with the fact that schoolwork overlapped into my own personal time at home. Due to my Asperger's, I needed a clear division between home and school.

Much of my stress was caused because the teachers failed to understand me and what I needed to feel comfortable. For example, on one particular school trip to the park when I was in Year 5 my mum told the teachers that I was really worried about going as I did not know what would be happening. They told my mum that it was the same for everyone, no one knew what would be happening, and they would not treat me any differently. My mum told the teacher that it was not the same for me as I had Asperger's. I was so worried about the trip that I was crying for ages the night before. I needed to know ahead of time exactly what we would be doing at the park to prepare myself mentally for it. Otherwise, I felt very panicky and as if things were out of control. All the teacher had to do was to explain the itinerary for the day and I would have felt a lot less stressed.

Some of the teachers would not accept that I should be treated any differently and, in my opinion, made as little effort as possible to do so. They thought that everyone should follow the same rules. I think that as they could not see my Asperger's, because it is a hidden disability, they thought that I should follow these rules like everyone else. Some teachers had a preconceived idea that people with Asperger's can't look you in the eye. However, I think that because I can look people in the eye, some teachers assumed that I did not have Asperger's. They were unaware that everyone with Asperger's is different, hence why Asperger's is referred to as a spectrum disorder. We are all different.

I used to think of school as a prison, and I once told my mum that I would rather be in a real prison than go to school. At least prisoners can do what they like in their cells. I used to suffer from extreme anxiety about school and the fact of having to be left there every day. An overwhelming feeling would come over me where I felt I just had to get out, away and back home. Sometimes I would stand by the school fence or gate and look into the outside world contemplating whether or not to run away. I never did run away from school, but I wanted to. I was once adamant that I couldn't go to school anymore and even talked about killing myself. I told my parents that I had done my time and could take it no longer. Another time my mum took me to the optician's, which meant that I was one hour late to school. At the opticians, I told her that at school I felt like I was trapped in a small box with teachers bossing me about. I felt free at the opticians but imprisoned at school. I also told my mum that I might as well shoot myself, escape over the school fence or go to the kitchen and stab myself.

I hated going to primary school. Just to get me in everyday was a huge struggle for my mum. In all honesty, I was really depressed at the time. My mum used to have to drag me into school every morning as I would be trying to drag her the other way. I would be shouting, crying, hitting and annoying my mum, trying to do anything I could to not have to go in. At home, I would get my school clothes on as late as possible and not until my mum started shouting at me. A lot of the time she would leave me with the Deputy Head who was very understanding and would try and calm me down. She eventually had a meeting with some of the teachers and said to them, "You wouldn't treat a dog like this, persistently dragging them to a place that stressed them. At what point do I stop bringing him in?"

Because of this my mum then had a reputation with some teachers as being a fussy mother!

One morning I was more stressed than usual, and I was in a terrible state walking to school and then waiting for the school doors to open. I was also feeling hungry, which always made me more stressed, and there was no time for me to stop and buy food at the shop. This tipped me over the edge. I lashed out with my book bag, which hit my mum on the head and really hurt her as it contained a metal pencil case. My mum ended up with a lump on her head and felt really upset and embarrassed. She was also worried about leaving me in such a state. When she got to work, she called the Deputy Head to ask if he could check that I was ok, as he was one of the few understanding people at the school. He came and spoke to me in the playground to make sure I was alright and played a game of Top Trumps with me, which he knew I enjoyed. He made me feel better, but I was still very remorseful for having hurt my mum.

Every morning and afternoon before school finished, I would meet with a Special Needs Assistant, who would talk to me about my problems and worries. She was instrumental in keeping me at school each day and calming me down every morning. I really needed to see her for one hour a day as five minutes was not long enough. It was even in my Statement that I would have one hour of additional support each day, but that rarely happened. I had a worry book where she and my mum would write about my worries and how I had been on particular days both at home and at school. Towards the end of my time at the school, she even helped me to count down the days I had left there! I also had a "time outs" system which allowed me, if I was feeling stressed, to go to a quiet place for five or ten minutes where I would read one of my football programmes. Football is one of my passions in life and at school it used to be a great outlet for my stress. Reading my football programmes took my mind off the worries and stresses I was experiencing and gave me another focus in life.

Sometimes in the afternoon I would not tell the Special Needs Assistant how I had been feeling during the day because I wanted to make sure that I left on time. One of the problems was that I used to feel like she was one of the teachers and my mum tried to tell me that she was not one of the teachers and that I should tell her exactly how I was feeling. I told my mum that sometimes my worries were so jumbled up in my head that I couldn't get them out. The child psychiatrist that I used to see from CAMHS said that it may be a good idea for her to come in and see the school SENCO with me so that she could help me to explain my worries better. Sometimes when I had a "time out" I would need to go and see the Special Needs Assistant, but one of the other teachers had told me not to disturb her during the day. For this reason, I used to worry about where to go for a "time out" and how long I could take. Consequently, the "time out" solution was not as effective as it could have been.

Remember to always have a contingency plan in case you are feeling stressed. Something that has helped me in times of stress is to have a contingency plan to take my mind off the stress e.g. reading a football programme or watching children's TV.

CHAPTER 3
Stories from my time at primary school

"Fewer than half of children and young people on the autism spectrum say they are happy at school."

National Autistic Society,
Autism and Education in England 2017

D ance was one of my least favourite subjects at primary school. In Years 5 and 6 we had dance lessons once a week for around half of each school year. This was compared to only one lesson of football. The school said that dance was compulsory, but my cousin who attended a different primary school did not even do dance. Even the other classes in my year did not do as much dance as we did, as they did other sports such as rounders instead. I hated these lessons; they were awful. For a start, I would rather have been doing more recognisable sports, such as football and tennis, which I really enjoyed. The dance teacher used to go far too fast for me to keep up with, and the modern pop music that she would play really used to irritate me. I would rather have done ballroom dancing like on *Strictly Come Dancing* than the fast hip hop kind of dances that we always used to do. As I did not like these lessons, I would always try and not join in, but then I would have girls in the class telling tales on me. This made me dislike the lessons even more.

Sometimes we had to do dance in the dinner hall right after lunch. The floor was still covered in bits of food and it was disgusting. People on the autistic spectrum are often over- or under- sensitive to sensory stimuli such as that of touch. I could not bear to feel the sensation of crumbs beneath my bare feet. The dance teacher could have helped by checking the floor was cleaned before the lesson. Once, I even had one of my friends rolling on top of me as it was part of the routine. I hated people touching me and I could not wait for this to be over. Many people with Asperger's do not like to be touched or hugged. It would have made my life a lot less stressful if the teacher would have allowed me to sit out of this routine and it would not have affected anyone else. Often the solutions to help Asperger's students are simple and have no consequence for other students; so why do teachers insist on ignoring them?

I also hated what was called the "buddy" system. This was a system where each pupil from Year 6 was paired up with someone from a lower year to look after them at lunchtime. It was also in place so that the younger pupil had someone older that they could talk to. The girls all seemed to like it, but most of the boys didn't. At lunchtime I just wanted to sit with my friends, but instead I had to sit with my "buddy". It felt like the teachers were taking away the one enjoyable part of the day. Luckily, I shared my buddy with one of the girls in my class, so most of the time I left her to look after him. It was also quite confusing because my buddy was a twin, so I never quite knew which one he was. Once when I was sitting in the dinner hall with my buddy I decided to go and sit by my friends on another table. As I got up, one of the dinner ladies who I really disliked told me to sit back down as I had to stay by my buddy.

I really did not like this particular dinner lady. She once made me eat my sandwich before my other items, which really annoyed me. I will never understand why she thought it was ok for her to be so bossy towards me! I also could not understand why she was allowed to shout at us and talk back to us but we were not allowed to shout or talk back to her. She once told one of my friends off for answering her back. She said to him, "Don't answer me back or I'll send you to the Headmistress." In this instance, I felt like shooting all of the teachers so that children would not have to be tortured anymore! I wrote down all the teachers that I hated and at the top of the paper I put, "Children are not teacher's slaves, stop treating us like we are." I could not accept that there was one rule for teachers and one rule for children, as in my opinion we are all human beings, aren't we? I felt as though I could not argue my corner with any of the teachers because they would have just said that I was cheeky and rude and I would get in trouble. People with Asperger's might often appear to be disrespectful to others. However, that's not the case; they can and do respect people immensely. But there has to be a good reason for that respect, and not just because you say so!

Whilst I was in Year 6, my last year at the school, there was a two-day school trip that most of my year were going on. I was really worried about this as I did not know what I would be doing and really did not want to spend my own time with the teachers – i.e. the evening and night time when I would normally be at home. I decided that I would not go on the trip. However, the school still insisted that I went into school, even though that would mean me being the only one from my year there. Instead, my dad decided that I would not be going in and so I had the two days off. School trips can cause an enormous amount of anxiety for children with Asperger's due to the number of unknowns – What will I eat? Where will I sleep? What will I do when I get there? etc.

One incident occurred when my whole year group were together in one classroom as we were all being handed letters. It was the end of the school day and as we were sitting there the bell rang. Luckily, I was by the door, so when the teachers were not looking, I just ran out as fast as I could to where my mum was. I always used to run as fast as I could to my mum every day after school as I knew that as soon as I got to her, I was free. It used to feel like I was escaping to freedom. As soon as the bell went for the end of the day it was my time and I did not want to stay at school for a second longer. My friend was sitting in the middle of the room and, as he used to have really bad anxiety, it must have felt awful for him having to stay behind. One teacher tried to give him his letter quickly but another teacher, who we felt used to bully us, made him wait his turn. I can only imagine how this made him feel as he suffered with his anxiety.

Every year we each had a peg in the cloakroom where we could hang our coats and bags. One year, my peg was right in the corner of the cloakroom, which meant that every time I arrived at school and left in the afternoon, I had to go right through everyone else (the crowd of people) which made me feel very uncomfortable as I can't stand being in crowded spaces. I was also being pushed and shoved by the hustle and bustle of the amount of people in the cloakroom, which just made the situation worse. It is well documented how people with Asperger's are generally very uncomfortable in crowded spaces, and considering that this was a daily problem, you can imagine how agitated it made me!

In one particular lesson we were making Mother's Day cards. To be honest, I did not see the point in them at the time and decided to draw football badges on my mum's card because that is what I liked. The teacher was going around the classroom looking at everyone's cards, and when she got to mine, she did not like it. She made me stick a piece of paper over the football badges and write a soppy "Roses are red" poem like all the girls in my class had done. I deliberately stuck the piece of paper on badly so that when I got to the cloakroom to put it in my bag, I could take the soppy poem out, which I did. My mum even told me that she would rather have the football badges on the card than the poem, anyway, as she knew this was what I had done and was genuine. It was very hard for me to do something that I did not see the point in. Drawing football badges on the card allowed me to be able to cope with the situation. I think this story highlights the lack of understanding that some teachers have when dealing with Asperger's students and also why there is a great need to educate teachers on the condition.

Some of the problems I was having at primary school could have very easily been resolved if they had been dealt with differently or by using different methods and approaches. For example, I was thrown into the deep end with dance, which is why I probably hated it so much. If the teachers had given me a staged approach where I was introduced to the lessons a little at a time, I may not have disliked it so much. Teachers used to tell me off in front of the whole year, but it would have been much less stressful for me to have been informed of any punishments on a one-to-one basis. Plus, I should have been told of any consequences in advance. This would have been a useful strategy to use for school trips. If I had known what we would be doing in advance, then it would have decreased my worries and anxiety. Again, it is because teachers are not adequately trained about Asperger's syndrome that they often are unaware of what is really upsetting us and are oblivious to the simple solutions that could make everybody's life easier!

"Adopting the right attitude can convert a negative stress into a positive one."

Hans Selye

CHAPTER 4
Being bullied

"34% of children on the autism spectrum say that the worst thing about being at school is being picked on."

The National Autistic Society, Autism facts and history

I n primary school I was not only bullied by some of the girls in my class but it also felt like I was bullied by some of the teachers! The girls were forever telling tales on my friend and me, and the teachers always believed them and told us off. It was a different story at my secondary school where the "tell-tales" would be told off by the teachers, but in my primary school they were thanked and encouraged. The girls used to tell on us for all manner of things, such as if we were trading football cards when they were banned, not singing in assembly or talking in class; and the teachers used to try and make an example of us. Even if the girls told on me for reading one of my football programmes in class, the teachers would still tell me off. This was despite the fact that they knew I was reading my programmes because I was stressed.

I used to play football most days at school, and when we were once told that we were banned from playing for two weeks I was very angry. I was in a terrible rage that night at home, telling everyone to shut their gobs and calling my mum a "dirty woman" and a "silly moron". I threatened to knock her out and told her that I wished she was dead. I even missed my football on the TV that night, which made me even worse. I went upstairs crying and was in such a rage. The best thing that you can do if your child is having a meltdown is to empathise with them or at least not to confront them. When they are having a meltdown they can't think straight, so there is no point telling them off or trying to find solutions. They will calm down eventually, but it is best for them to do this naturally and in their own time. This is very difficult for carers to do, but try it and I am sure you will see the benefit of this approach.

The reason that we were banned from playing football was because some of the players, not including myself, had been playing roughly. During one of the two weeks that we were banned, most of the year were on a school trip, and so my friend and I decided to play football. When the year returned from the trip a group of girls told our teacher about us and the teacher got the whole year together and told everyone, making me feel like the culprit. She said, "There is one person letting us down and he knows who he is," and "Don't bother bringing in a policeman, or a lawyer or your mum, dad and grandparents or anyone else because you'll still have your punishment." I replied, "What about Tony Blair?" It was the first time I had defended myself against the teachers. I thought that the girls hated my friend and me, and my friend even said to me, "Do you know we are the most hated in the class?" The teacher then got the year together for a second time so that they could watch me being told off, and they were all asked what my punishment should be. I was very upset over the injustice of punishing the whole school for the actions of a few boys. I didn't see why I had to stop playing football anyway, but to have the teachers try to humiliate me in front of the whole class gave me a terrible sense of isolation.

A similar event had occurred the previous year when I wore my trainers into school. My mum had already explained to the teacher that I had sensory issues as a result of my Asperger's and that I did not like the feel of my school shoes. I don't think the teacher was listening because she got the whole year group together and asked them, "Who would like to wear trainers to school?" I felt like the teacher was just trying to make me look stupid.

One day my friend and I were told tales on by a group of five girls. The girls told tales on us for talking in assembly, and as a result of this one of the teachers came and sat next to us. Afterwards, she said that she was very disappointed and that she wanted us to say sorry to the girls. She said she would check if we had said sorry. Why should I say sorry to someone if I have done nothing wrong? We were also made to feel like we had to put our hands up and admit to being moaners when she asked the year group who they thought were "a bit of a moaner". We also got told off for going to see the Deputy Head. He had told my friend that he could come and speak to him anytime. He was far more understanding than the Headteacher, and I think my time at the school would have been a lot less stressful if he had been the headteacher.

It got to the point where I felt that some of my friends had even started turning on me. When the teacher had asked what my punishment should be regarding the football ban it was not only the girls but also some of the boys who started to make suggestions, some of whom were my friends! Also, when the ban was lifted and we were allowed to play again I feared that they would not accept me back. Luckily, they did and I was able to play again. Some of my friends had also started doing things such as taking the mickey out of me about the way I ran and spoke, poking me repeatedly, which I can't bear, and putting grass down my back.

Sometimes I did not even know when I was being bullied. This is typical of people with Asperger's because we have difficulty knowing who is a friend. We often find it hard to distinguish banter from bullying for example. My dad said that I was like Pinocchio going off to school and I had to be careful of characters like Foulfellow and Gideon, the sly fox, because I was naïve and could be easily misled. Often, I did not understand who my friends were and who the bullies were. My dad remembers when one of my friends from primary school came round to our house and I was talking to him about some of my friends. My friend said, "No, Alex, they're not your friends; they are always bullying you." My dad asked my friend how and he then explained some of the things they had done. I did not even know that these things were meant in a nasty way and were a form of bullying!

It was not only the girls in our year that bullied us but it often felt like some of the teachers did too. One teacher who, in my opinion, used to bully us once threatened to make us stand up in assembly and admit that we were the reason why the football cards had been banned. He said to us, "Better hope there is not an assembly tomorrow or I will get you out in front of everyone and explain you're the reason for the ban." Straight after the assembly, I had a "time out" and went and cried a lot because I just felt like beating this teacher up badly. He also tried to make us lie to our parents. However, when our parents came in and spoke to the teacher about the incident, he denied everything. On a trip to the park in 2007, a piece of fruit went missing and the first person the teacher (albeit a different teacher this time) accused was me. I felt a great amount of injustice at my primary school. I believe that some teachers didn't recognise my Statement of Special Educational Needs or my Asperger's and ignored the advice in my Statement on how to best handle me. This made my life at primary school very miserable.

At my secondary school the bullying was not an everyday occurrence and was not nearly as bad as it had been before at primary school. Unfortunately, I was still bullied a little bit. There was one particular boy in my year who would often bother me. He was always getting into trouble for various things, and I think he should have been kicked out of the school in Year 7. I recall in one table tennis lesson that he was cheating as usual. I always used to beat him as I was one of the best in my year. Our rule was that losers moved down a table, but he refused to and insisted that I move down instead of him. Later on in the school, again during P.E. lessons, he would still be bothering me and some of my friends. He would be saying things to us that used to really upset and annoy us. We told the teachers, and they must have discussed this matter with him as he didn't bother us so much again. It's a shame that my primary school teachers didn't adopt the same approach!

Another problem I had at secondary school was that the P.E. changing rooms were awful; they were so small and cramped and you could not really fit everyone in. I used to dread going in there as we literally had no room. In the end, two of my friends and I were allowed to change around the corner by the fitness suite. At least this demonstrated the teachers' understanding of our problem and they offered us a solution. Although this was not an ideal solution, we did appreciate their help. Again, this shows how much teachers can help Asperger's students if they understand, listen and take appropriate action.

"You can't stop the waves, but you can learn to surf!"

Jon Kabat-Zinn

CHAPTER 5
Mental health

"As of December 2016, the UK prison population stood at 84,069. Let's say that 1 per cent of prisoners have ASDs – the same prevalence as in the general population – then there are at least 840 prisoners who are on the spectrum."

The Independent, Wednesday, 18th January 2017

As soon as I was "statemented" in 2007 I started to see a consultant child psychiatrist in the "Child and Family Unit" at CAMHS in our local health centre. I saw her regularly from 2007-2009 until she left. She really understood me, my challenges and struggles, and was a great help not only to myself but also to my family. When she left, I went to see another two child psychiatrists but, unfortunately, I felt that they did not understand me at all. In our first meeting with them we told them about the things that used to get me stressed and that used to calm me down. One of the things we told them was that chocolate calmed me down if I was stressed or having a meltdown. They thought that I was manipulating my parents just so that I could have some chocolate! I didn't eat that much chocolate anyway and my parents would have bought it for me regardless. After one meeting with them we decided not to go again as they clearly did not understand me. That was the last time that I went to the "Child and Family Unit", which was a shame as I could have done with their help, especially during my later years at secondary school when I suffered from increased anxiety.

The child psychiatrist we saw from 2007 to 2009 had a deep understanding of me, my family and my problems, and had gained my trust and respect. She used to help me to deal with all of the problems and worries I was having at school and at home and help me and my family to find suitable solutions. She would regularly send emails and liaise with the SENCO at my school and would often tell me stories about some of the other people that she had to see, some of whom were in prison!

The majority of issues that we spoke to the child psychiatrist about revolved either around school or family. The problems I had at home were often a result of my time at school. Often, children with Asperger's syndrome will seem to be coping at school and will seem to be calm, but when they get home, they let their anxieties out by being aggressive and angry. I would always say sorry to my parents after being angry, and the psychiatrist told us that this was a really good sign. Saying sorry showed that I cared as she told us that some of the people she saw did not care about their actions. Also, at school I did not act like I did at home because I was scared of the consequences of getting a detention, and so we talked about why it was important not to get angry. On our last meeting with her we spoke about my desire to join the school football team, the way I insist on having things immediately, my intelligence and about how I feel emotionally. My dad remembers that she often used to tell me that I was intelligent and therefore had the resources to solve my own problems, such as anger. She seemed to always have a smart way of getting me to think positively and think for myself.

In 2009, I got a prescription for medication (0.25ml daily of fluoxetine hydrochloride) from the child psychiatrist at CAMHS. The medication made me feel calmer in the mornings and at bedtime but no better at school. I took this medication for about a year until my dad wanted to see how I would be without it. They told my dad at CAMHS to give me my medication every other day for three weeks and then for him to stop giving it to me. That is exactly what my dad did and I seemed to be ok afterwards.

I used to suffer from extreme anxiety about school and the fact of having to be left there every day. An overwhelming feeling would come over me where I felt I just had to get out, away and back home. I remember the first day back at secondary school after one particular summer holiday. The first thing that we did that day was to have an assembly and I felt so stressed that I actually felt sick. During the summer I had been to a WWT (Wildfowl and Wetlands Trust) bird centre in Wales with my grandparents and had bought a pink wristband from the shop. I kept looking at this during the assembly and thinking about my holiday. My mental health was also affected by all the changes that were introduced by the Headteacher during my GCSE years at secondary school. During the first half of Year 11, I was in a total mess and so stressed that I thought my GCSEs would be affected. Luckily, I managed to turn my attitude to school around. I was determined to achieve good grades in my GCSEs. Maybe the psychiatrist's advice all those years earlier, on how to solve problems myself, helped me use my anger towards this Headteacher in a positive way?

I also have something called palilalia, which is a speech disorder that involves me involuntarily repeating words and phrases in a whisper. I don't repeat everything that I say, just the last four or five words of a sentence. My family were the ones who started to notice me repeating words as I did not know that I did. The louder my voice is or the more stressed I am then the louder and more obvious my palilalia will be. I can't control this, but it does not really affect or bother me at all; it's just something that I have. Palilalia is quite common in people who have autism and Asperger's and is often an indication that a child is not acquiring or using verbal communication in a neurotypical fashion.

"Health is better than wealth!"

Kresha

CHAPTER 6
Meltdowns

"A meltdown is 'an intense response to overwhelming situations'. It happens when someone becomes completely overwhelmed by their current situation and temporarily loses behavioural control. This loss of control can be expressed verbally (e.g. shouting, screaming, crying), physically (e.g. kicking, lashing out, biting) or in both ways."

The National Autistic Society, Meltdowns

Sometimes, when I used to come home from school, one very small incident, which most people would probably not have thought twice about, would make me go mad with anger or stress. My parents would be wondering how such a small incident could get me so angry or stressed. However, it would be a series of seven or eight incidents that would have happened over the school day and that one last little thing, such as my sister saying something to me or dropping something on the floor, will have made that last little piece of string inside me snap. I just could not think of anything else or see any way out of the anger and stress. After about one hour I would usually go to my room and just cry, as I did not want to get angry at my parents but saw no other way of dealing with my stresses. Two things that used to calm me down and relieve the stress were chocolate and children's television. Although I didn't eat a lot of sweets, chocolate used to help me as I used to be that little bit more frustrated when I was hungry and so it just took that frustration out of me. I have always liked watching children's television, and as soon as my mum put on a children's programme, I used to instantly feel relaxed. All the stresses and worries would just go in an instant and I would become glued to the television like in a trance. It must have felt like magic to my parents!

When I was angry, I used to shout at my parents calling them every name under the sun and nagging and nagging them about certain things or constantly saying that I wanted something doing this instant. It was most often my mum who I directed my anger and stress at, and it would last for about an hour. Some autistic people break or throw things when they are angry, but I never did that. I could not bring myself to break anything as I knew how bad I would have felt afterwards. After I had returned home from one holiday with my grandparents in Wales I got in to a terrible rage, demanding that the holiday photos were developed straight away. I was punching myself and my computer keyboard, thumping the settee, calling my mum a "moron" etc.

I was depressed about getting older, people dying, worrying about going up to Year 8 and the Easter holiday being a third over. I told my mum that I was interested in Asperger's schools if they were not too far away and asked if I could take a pill to make myself happy! I also told her that sport makes me feel better. For a short while at my secondary school I had a pillow kept in one of the cupboards in case I was angry. I could then let all my anger out on the pillow, but I only ever used it a handful of times.

On my 13th birthday I had been having a lovely day with my Uncle Tim. As he was leaving my house, I started to get really angry because I could not find a TV to watch the football on. My sister agreed to let me watch it in her room, but she insisted that my mum sat with me. Although my mum had given me some of my medication, I still went mad over this by shouting, swearing and hitting the TV. I calmed down quite quickly, though, and was very apologetic. I told my mum that I did not want to get so stressed and angry and that it was probably because I had school the next day and the fact that my birthday was nearly over that I got into such a state. I was very upset and said that I needed help and that at the time I just couldn't think about anything else other than what was upsetting me. I couldn't think logically when I was like this.

I used to become angry over a variety of different things, and it was usually something else that was bothering or worrying me and not the thing it appeared that I was stressed about. In a coffee shop I once got really annoyed over a voucher for some football cards that was in one of the newspapers. I could not get the voucher because another woman was reading the paper and I had an absolute fit. Once, the morning after I had got into a state the night before, I told my dad that I had watched a programme on TV and there were situations where one person was having a fit and the other one slapped them and they snapped out of it. I told him that I thought he needed to do that to me. (He never did though!) I also used to get really angry with my youngest sister. She never used to say anything to me, but she used to make a lot of mess around the house. Mess is one of the triggers that can cause me to have a meltdown and her mess used to drive me crazy.

From a very young age I have always had trouble with messy environments; I just can't seem to function in them. If I am in a messy environment, then my mind is messy and I just can't think straight. Similarly, if I am in a tidy environment, then my mind is clear and ordered and I feel like I can do anything. Imagine being trapped in the middle of a landfill site and not being able to get out. Well, that is how I feel in a messy or untidy environment. It feels as though the mess is creeping up on me to the point where I feel trapped.

Messy environments are one of the triggers that can lead me to having a meltdown. For a lot of people, a meltdown can result in them getting very angry, shouting or just running away as fast as they can. For me, I just get so overwhelmed that I go to a quiet place, usually my bedroom if I am at home, and start crying. Once, I was at home in my kitchen, which at the best of times is still very messy, and found myself having a meltdown. I just stopped what I was doing and ran straight up to my room crying. I phoned my mum, who was downstairs, and she was really concerned that something bad had happened. She even thought that someone must have died, due to how upset I was. When I told her that I was upset by the kitchen being messy she just burst out laughing. In all honesty, she did make me feel a bit better then as I realised what a silly thing it was to get so upset about!

Another meltdown I had recently was again when I was in my kitchen. However, this time it was not because it was messy as for once it was actually quite tidy. I was unloading the dishwasher and things were going wrong. First of all, I could not fit the wooden spoons into the correct drawer as it would not close. Then, when I tried to put the mugs back in the mug cupboard there was no room. Someone had put glasses in the mug cupboard instead of in the glass cupboard. Some of the items I did not even know where they went. But the last straw was when a pool of water spilt on the floor from a jug handle. I instantly felt like I needed to get out of the kitchen, but as I only had the cutlery to put away, I did this as fast as I could before running up to my bedroom. That was probably not the best of ideas as I should have gone to my room straightaway. To calm myself down I watched a DVD of *Cloudbabies*, a show on CBeebies.

I never felt like I could be myself at school and was never able to fully express how I was feeling to anyone. Whilst I trusted one or two teachers at my secondary school, I still did not feel as though I could tell them everything. My parents were the only ones that I could truly open up to and express how I was actually feeling. This is why I would get so angry when I got home from school. I would essentially be bottling everything up until I got home.

"Sometimes good things fall apart so better things can fall together!"

Marilyn Monroe

CHAPTER 7
My family

"A child with autism also influences his or her neurotypical siblings. The siblings undergo many of the stresses faced by the other family members. Moreover, parents may not be able to provide them with full support, as they are overwhelmed meeting the needs and demands of their autistic child."

PsychCentral,
Four ways a child with autism affects family life

My family have been a huge help and without them I would probably have been a lot worse and had a lot more problems. I am fortunate that I have a very large family, including eighteen cousins, eight uncles and six aunts, so I can always call someone or get away from my own house if I am stressed or having problems. When I was younger, I was always ringing up my Uncle Tim, who would be able to talk over my problems with me and calm me down. It was like a lifeline and he always made me feel calmer. Tim is not technically my real uncle; he is my dad's best friend from school. However, as soon as I was born, we became very close and have stayed that way ever since. Just like with my Uncle Tim, I had the same strategy with my dad when I was at secondary school. I hated school and used to feel like school was a prison. Sometimes all I wanted to do was get out to, as I called it, "the outside world", even if it was just for five minutes. As we were not allowed out until the end of the day, I used to always phone my dad when I was stressed. It made me feel as though I was communicating with the outside world, and I knew he was the one person who was always available to talk to. A number of my friends who have Asperger's don't have a large family like I do and so do not have that extra support that I have found invaluable. Even to this day, if I ever become stressed, then I can always go around to my grandad's or my uncles or just give them a call, which always helps to relieve my stress.

I have two younger sisters, one who is just a year younger than me and one who is four years younger than me. From the moment my first sister was born I did not get on with her, and my parents remember that I would constantly be saying "No, No" to her. As I have got older, my relationship with my sisters has not got any better and in some respects it has got worse. In all honesty, it would have been easier if I had been an only child! It's never easy for siblings of an autistic child as the child with autism sometimes demands most of the parents' attention. My sisters became so fed up with me that they found ways to push my buttons. If I was angry and just at the stage where I was calming down, they would say something to me that they knew would make my anger go through the roof. I would end up being angrier than I was in the first place.

My Uncle Tim is one person who I can always rely on to calm me down whenever I am stressed. Like many people with Asperger's, I have a subject that I am obsessed with, and mine is football. My Uncle Tim always took me to football matches on the weekends up and down the country, and this was a huge stress reliever. If I was ever stressed at school, I could always think about recent trips that I had had with him to different matches and grounds or look forward to upcoming matches. Tim always bought me a programme from each and every match that we attended, and if ever I was feeling a little stressed or panicky during the school day, I would have somewhere quiet that I could go to have a read of my programmes.

My Grandad Doug, who I call Poppa, has also been someone who has played a huge part in my life. Every Friday evening, without fail, I would go and stay the night at his house after school, which gave me something to look forward to. I would also go to his house every Monday evening for my weekly squash lesson with my cousin. As I have become older and have started my own business creating promotional videos and carrying out talks on my Asperger's, I have started to stay at his house more often, some weeks spending more time at his house than at my own. I find his house more relaxing than my own house as it is quieter and tidier; plus my sisters are never there to annoy me.

When I was diagnosed with Asperger's my dad told me that other people in our family had it as well and that we were very fortunate to have Asperger's. He also told me that having Asperger's made us positively different from everyone else, with for example, the ability to think creatively and the determination to achieve our goals. It is believed that Asperger's can be passed down through and run in families, and this may be part of the reason why I have it. My Grandad Gordon is an example of one member of my family who is, in some ways, eccentric and I think has a few traits of Asperger's. I have always got on really well with him and I am just like him in many ways, such as the clothes that I wear and the music that I listen to. I always say that he is part of the reason why I like colourful clothes as he wears a lot of bright shirts, ties and blazers. We often enjoy going shopping together and singing all of his old 50s rock and roll songs around the supermarket. I really enjoy his company and he has always been there as another option for me to call or visit when I am feeling stressed. As I have already mentioned, I have been very fortunate to have such a large support network.

"What really matters is what you do with what you have."   H G Wells

CHAPTER 8
Holidays

"Going on holiday with a child or adult on the autism spectrum can be a challenging prospect. There are a number of reasons why this might be the case. There may be issues with adapting to change, to a new environment or in supporting the individual to manage various forms of transport, new routines and new activities."

Scottish Autism, Going on holiday

As a child, I was very lucky as I went on many holidays with my family. Every year we used to have a holiday in Cornwall as well as a holiday on the South Coast in Lyme Regis. Also, my grandparents used to take me to Wales every year and my parents would often take me and my sisters to Disneyland Paris and Walt Disney World Florida. Also, my Uncle Tim took me on a few holidays to Torquay. Although I really enjoyed each and every holiday that I went on, I still had Asperger's! This meant that, whilst I was far more relaxed, I could still get stressed very easily and still had worries and problems which all stemmed from my Asperger's.

Holidays can be a big source of stress for people with Asperger's because, although they are meant to be fun, it is a change to their normal routine.

Every year we used to go down to Cornwall with our family. There would be about fifteen of us, including my grandma, lots of my aunts, uncles, cousins and my parents and two sisters. We used to go and see my great aunt who lives in Cornwall, and when we first used to go and visit, we would stay at her house. As we got older, we used to stay in some holiday cottages with our cousins. The holiday cottages were part of a country park, and every evening in the bar they would put on games for the children. They even hosted a talent show and one year I won it. I sang "I Can See Clearly Now" by Johnny Nash. I am very bad at singing, and my dad and uncle in particular were in fits of laughter during the performance. Not only could you hear them on the video but you could tell how funny they found it as the footage was so shaky. At the time, I was oblivious and not at all nervous doing it. Unfortunately, both of the recordings of my performance have been lost.

They also had a swimming pool in the complex, and whilst I liked going in the pool, I hated the changing rooms. My youngest cousins used to find me hilarious as I was always calling the floor of the changing rooms "gross grot". It seemed so old and dirty as you could see bits of hair and grit from people's shoes that I did not want to touch it with my bare feet. For this reason, I would always wear beach shoes into the pool. I also had a similar feeling about the beach as I hated the sand, not so much the feel of it but the way it stuck to your toes and got in your shoes. If I had walked on the beach in my shoes, then no matter how long I had spent trying to get the sand out of them I could still feel sand in my shoes for weeks afterwards.

A lot of the time I would prefer to go shopping with my great aunt and my grandma than to go to the beach with my cousins. This was partly because I did not want to get sand in my shoes, but also because, in some respects, I felt like an adult as I liked to do adult things and eat adult foods. My dad remembers going into one shop and the lady saying, "Hello Alex," as she remembered me from the year before. However, because I always had two choices, going to the beach or going shopping, it used to pose quite a problem. Even though I always knew what my cousins would be doing, I would get really stressed and panicky if I did not know what the rest of my family were doing. The rest of my family would often do their own thing, and each morning I would ring them up to see where they were going. Sometimes I wanted to do both of the things, i.e. to go shopping *and* go to the beach, and whatever I decided I was always worried I had missed out on something more exciting. People with Asperger's often find making decisions difficult as they panic about making the wrong choice. Therefore, it is a good idea to limit the number of choices where possible.

Once, when I went shopping with my family in Cornwall, my dad bought me a ukulele from a local music shop. Afterwards we went for a coffee and I decided to stand outside the coffee shop and do some busking. I had never even played a ukulele before, but I did manage to get a bit of money from passers-by. My nan and great aunt were in hysterics, and my dad captured the performance on video. One of my sisters was so jealous that I was making some money that she said, "I want some money," so my dad had to go back to the shop and buy her a recorder so that she could join in. To be honest, I did not really want her to join in!

We also have some friends who live in Bournemouth, the same ones who we went to see in America and who initially suspected that I had Asperger's. We used to go and visit them occasionally but not every year. On one holiday in Bournemouth we stayed in a really posh hotel. One evening we decided that we would all go out for dinner in the hotel's restaurant. The service was awful and some of my family either had to wait ages for their meal or got the wrong meal. My aunt went to complain, but after hearing me sum up everything that was wrong, she let me tell them what had happened. I kept saying to the hotel manager, "That's not right," one of my favourite sayings, and explaining all the things that were wrong with the meal. My dad said that he couldn't have handled the situation as well as I did, and as a consequence the hotel manager gave us the meal free and offered us another free meal the next night! My parents remember how I often would say, "That's not right," about all sorts of things and was so angry once that I wrote a letter to the then Prime Minister, Tony Blair, complaining about our experience. When I was younger, I used to complain about hills and even wanted to write to the Prime Minister to let him know how much I hated them and how they should all be flattened!

Whenever we went anywhere as a family, I would always insist on sitting in the front of the car so that I did not have to sit with my sisters in the back. I never got on with them and just sitting next to them was bad enough. At school, I hated having school photos because they always insisted on getting one of me with my sisters and I would always have to sit far too close to them for my liking (fortunately they did not go to my secondary school!) On holidays my dad was always trying to separate me and my sisters to try and keep the peace. That is why it was always good when we went on holiday with a lot of our family, because whilst my sisters did one thing with my cousins, I could do another thing with the rest of my family. My dad said his strategy was to "divide and conquer"!

Wherever we went on holiday, I would always ask if we could go and visit one of the local football clubs. In Cornwall my dad once took me to watch Truro City. He did not come to the game himself, but he had arranged a day out to Truro on that particular day just so that I could go to the match. We have some friends in Wimbledon who we would often stay with. During our many visits there, my dad and his friend took me to watch England at Wembley, Chelsea and AFC Wimbledon. On one of the visits to see them my dad had told me that he would take me to see a local football club on the way home. As we were about to leave, my sister started saying things to me that were really winding me up. My parents would not listen, and to try and get her back I spat on her bag, which afterwards I felt really bad about. I did not want my friends to see me acting like this, but I felt that was the only way to get her back. My dad got so cross with me that he told me that we would not be visiting the football club anymore. My sister had got what she wanted as she hated football and did not want to visit the club. I felt a total sense of injustice as it felt like she had won. I was so angry that I had been punished as a result of my sister annoying me.

I was in a terrible state on the journey home. When we had travelled too far to visit the club all I wanted to do was to get home as fast as we could so that I could go and see my grandparents. On the way home, we stopped off in Marlow and I decided that I would walk to see Marlow Rugby Club to try and cool down. It was about two miles to the club, but at the time I did not know this and to be honest did not care. I would have carried on walking even if it had been five miles. I also spoke to my Uncle Tim on the phone, who, as always, was able to calm me down and talk over the situation.

"Love the life you have while you create the life of your dreams."

Hal Elrod

CHAPTER 9
Moving to secondary school

"70% of children with autism are educated in mainstream schools; the rest are in specialist provisions (which isn't necessarily a bad thing: different environments suit different children)."

Ambitious About Autism, Stats and facts

As I had been diagnosed with Asperger's relatively young, when I was ten, it meant that I could choose the secondary school that was the most appropriate for me. As it turned out, I attended a small private school in Birmingham which had provisions in place to help people with Asperger's and autism. In fact, it was the only school that my parents put down on the form as it was the only appropriate school for people like myself. Family Equip, the charity I am involved with, had suggested the school because they had a large number of the charity's members with Asperger's who went there. The SENCO at the school was by far the best person my dad spoke to at any of the schools he visited and came across as very caring and knowledgeable. She reassured him that if I attended the school, then I would be looked after. My parents had thought about sending me to the primary section of the school a year earlier, meaning I would have been at the school from Year 6. However, although I hated my primary school, I still had a lot of friends there and did not want to leave them just yet.

The council had sent my dad to look around a few other schools. One school which was in Coventry had a large number of blind students as well as autistic students. My dad did not feel that this school was appropriate for me, and also he felt it was too far away. In addition, my dad visited a number of local schools. One of these schools was a large secondary school that had an Asperger's section, but when my dad saw so many students coming out of the classrooms at breaktime, he felt that this school would not be appropriate for me, even though he was very impressed with the Headmaster there. At my local catchment school, they suggested that I would be better off at another school, saying they would have more experience. It appeared that they did not want to be burdened with looking after someone who had Asperger's. (Interestingly, one of my friends who was later diagnosed with Asperger's went to this school; he had a terrible time there and hated it!)

One school they sent my dad to in Birmingham left him extremely upset. He told me that it was one of the most unnerving experiences he has ever had and he still thinks about it to this day! The school had pupils with autism and other severe mental health problems, and as my dad was in the waiting room, he witnessed a really big guy come bursting through the doors with staff chasing after him. They told my dad there was a special group who all had Asperger's and asked my dad to have a look into one of the classrooms. As he peered through the window, one boy jumped at the door and it made my dad jump backwards. It upset him so much that he called up the council as he left and told them that this kind of school would be inappropriate for me and he should not have been sent there.

My friend who had not been diagnosed with Asperger's at the time had to go to his local state school, which he hated. It was a very large school with over 1,000 pupils and was probably too big for him to cope with. His year group was the same size as my whole school. To give you a comparison, I thought that my secondary school was far better than my primary school. However, my friend thought that our primary school was better than his secondary school. He was eventually diagnosed with Asperger's, but not till a few years later.

I was not worried about starting secondary school. In fact, the only thing that I was worried about was having to go in for an induction day during the summer holidays (that was my time!) I had a smaller class size, teachers who understood me better and friends who also had autism and Asperger's who I felt that I could relate to. From Year 7 to Year 9, I was in what was known as the "small group" for core subjects (English and maths). Most of the people in the group had Asperger's like myself and the group gave us a smaller class, between seven and ten of us, compared to about twenty in the other classes, and more help. Right up until my last year at the school in the sixth form, I always had a teaching assistant in my class. When I was in the small group, we often had two teaching assistants and sometimes even three. The smaller class sizes were invaluable as we were given more one-on-one support. Whilst I found my secondary school much better than my primary school, I still disliked school and still had many struggles and worries. I think that I disliked my primary school so much that in some ways it just became a habit that I did not like school.

The small group were taught by a teacher who I really did not like. She was always giving us homework, which was a big problem of mine, was really strict and her lessons were just really boring. In one particular lesson she had to go out of the room for a while and as a bit of fun she left me in charge. When she came back in someone said that she should give me a detention and I told them that we don't have detentions or homework in my class. I had the same teaching assistant throughout six of the seven years that I was at the school. Whilst she could be strict at times, she was one of the only teachers in the school that I could fully trust. It was so reassuring to have someone in most of my lessons who I could go to for help or if I was stressed about something.

I never felt that I could be myself at school and was never able to fully express how I was feeling to anyone. If a number of incidents had got me stressed at school, then I would bottle them all up until I got home. Then any little incident at home would make me go mad with rage. It was like the last little piece of string inside me had snapped. At my primary school I did not trust any of the teachers. Whilst in comparison I trusted one or two teachers at my secondary school, I still did not feel as though I could tell them everything. My parents were the only ones that I could truly open up to and express how I was actually feeling. This is why I would get so angry when I got home from school.

Soon after I started secondary school, our year group went on a trip to Malvern for a few days to stay in an activity camp. At primary school I would never have gone on a trip like this because I could not have tolerated being with the teachers overnight and for that length of time. However, because I liked my new school more, I decided to go. Whilst we were there each room was shared by two people. Because my mum had told the school that I could not get to sleep if there were any noises, they gave me my own room. (I don't think my primary school would have done this.) Whilst in Malvern, we walked up to the highest point on the Malvern Hills, went walking through a quarry and carried out other activities. When I was in Year 10, I went on another school trip to France where we went to a waterpark, a theme park and a hypermarket. I enjoyed this trip being with my friends and I felt that I was well looked after.

Towards the end of my time at secondary school my dad encountered a lot of problems with the council, especially regarding the new Headteacher. However, the council not only paid for my school fees but they also provided me with a taxi to and from school with other people from my local area who also had Asperger's. The school was the nearest school that catered for people with autism and Asperger's, which is why I went there. I lived about nine miles away from the school and the taxi journey used to take about one hour there and one hour back, each and every day. When I first started the school there was just one taxi going from my area, but when I left the school there were about four taxis going from there. This just shows the number of people with autism and Asperger's who were at the school.

"Happiness is not something you postpone for the future; it is something you design for the present."

Jim Rohn

CHAPTER 10
The taxi

"Unexpected changes when taking public transport can be overwhelming. 79% of autistic people tell us they feel socially isolated, and for some, the fear of unexpected changes could mean not even leaving the house."

National Autistic Society, Accessing public transport

The children who travelled with me in my taxi changed slightly over the years as well as the drivers and guides. However, there were always about five of us in the taxi. When I first joined the school there was one particular girl in my taxi who always used to put Capital Radio on as she always sat in the front. I could not stand this radio station as I hated modern music and it used to drive me round the bend. This was before I had an iPhone or music player, so I had no way to solve the problem. In the end, one of the teachers had to ask the driver if we could have a rota so we did not have Capital Radio on the whole time. Eventually, my Uncle Tim bought me an MP3 player which I would listen to when this radio station was on.

There were a few people in my taxi who made the journey unpleasant. For example, a person being overweight meant that if you sat with them in the front of the taxi you literally had no room whatsoever. Another issue was a student having bad hygiene problems. It was not just me who noticed this but everyone else in the taxi, and as a consequence nobody ever wanted to sit by that person. As I mentioned, the people in the taxi changed over the years, and I can honestly say that everyone else was one of my friends. I had three different drivers throughout my time at the school and numerous guides. They were all very kind and friendly. One of my friends who went on another taxi said to me once, "Why do you always get the nice drivers?"

The first driver and guide that I had at the school were husband and wife and were the nicest people that you could ever meet. In fact, they were like an extended family. If I was stressed going into school in the mornings, they would always try and help me to calm down. Each year the taxi companies had to bid to decide if they would be working for the school again. My dad was really concerned in case we had a new driver who was not as nice or understanding. In fact, we did not possibly think that we could ever get a driver and guide as nice as those two. However, we were wrong. The second driver that I had was a really nice old man who was just as nice as my first driver and would also help me to calm down and de-stress in the mornings.

For the last three years at the school I can honestly say that the taxi journeys were the best part of the day and I would rather have been in the taxi than have had more time at home. Instead of going into school stressed, I would go into school a lot calmer as I had had time to unwind with my friends and the driver who was very funny. My friends and I were often playing silly games on the taxi like who could wave to the most people and who could spot the greatest number of sofas outside houses. I had the same driver for the last three years at the school, from Year 11 up until sixth form. I still keep in contact with him to this day, even though it has been four years since I left the school.

The number of people in the taxi meant you sometimes had to wait five or ten minutes for one person, even if everyone else had come out quickly. One of my friends in the taxi was regularly held back after lessons by his teacher, who also happened to be my form tutor. It was happening on a regular basis and was making me late for my weekly squash lesson. Sometimes I even had to miss my squash lesson which had already been paid for. As it was happening on a regular basis, my taxi driver reported this to the receptionist and to one of the teachers. My teaching assistant had also spoken to this teacher but had no success. On one occasion I went to the taxi and my driver asked me where my friend was. I told him that I thought I knew, so he told me to go quickly to get him. I went to his class to ask if he could be let out and I was asked to leave. I was very cross. I saw no other way to resolve the problem as other methods had failed, so I had taken the matter in to my own hands.

I still keep in touch and see some of my friends who were in my taxi whilst I was in sixth form. One of them only lives down the road from me. If we were ever early to school, we would go and play table tennis in the Den. We did this for a few months before one of the teachers tried to stop us. It used to calm us down and relax us in the mornings and made us start the day happier. I could see no reason why she was stopping us from playing. She told us that it was because there was nobody to supervise us but, let's face it, I was a sixth former and to be honest I think she was being deliberately awkward as no other teacher had a problem with us playing. Even though she kept telling us off, we kept going to play in the mornings. Also, three of us used to play table tennis every lunchtime and sometimes if I had a free period I would go and play with some of my other friends from my year.

"The journey of a thousand miles begins with one step."

Lao Tzu

CHAPTER 11
Secondary school

"It's quite common for autistic children who do not appear to have any behavioural difficulties at school to behave differently at home … Just because the difficult behaviour occurs at home, does not necessarily mean the trigger (or the cause) lies there. The child may find school very stressful, but keep their emotions locked up until they get home."

National Autistic Society,
Different behaviour between school and home

The school lunches at secondary school were horrible. When I started at the school, you were only allowed a packed lunch if you had a medical or religious reason. I could understand if you had a medical reason but a religious reason was out of choice and I could not understand how they were allowed to have packed lunches as well. This is because I am very logical and if something is not logical, then often I can't accept or understand it. When I first attended an open day at the school, whilst I was still at primary school, they had put on a really nice lunch. Because of this, we all thought that the food would be really nice at the school, but it was far from it. They used to serve hard pizza, always the same boring Margherita or pepperoni, packet mash potato and powdered eggs. I never used to eat much of the lunches, so my mum always packed me a sandwich in my bag. I had to hide in one of the school corridors to eat it in case I was seen and told off. Sometimes the queue for lunch was so long that you spent most of your lunchtime in the dinner hall. In the end, the school became a bit more lenient about packed lunches and so allowed me to have my own packed lunch. All throughout my time at school I used to have a strict number of items in my lunchbox. In primary school it was five items, but in secondary school it was only three. This was just part of my daily routine. It was part of the day which I could control and gave me structure and order.

Throughout my time at the school they always had a lunch club. When I started at the school, it used to be in the exam room and was set up for people who either did not want to go outside or who wanted to be in a quiet environment. We were able to play board games, go on the computer and play on the whiteboards. There was also a room called "Study Skills" where a lot of the teaching assistants used to go during breaks and lunchtime. This was another place where some of the students used to go, again to be in a quiet environment or if they wanted to do their homework. From Year 11 onwards, Lunch Club was moved and became what was called "the Den". In the Den we had a wider variety of activities. We still had computers and board games, but we also had table tennis and dodgeball in the small courtyard outside the room. I always used to go to lunch club and the Den.

In Year 8, my second year at the school, I had a friend who was in the year below. I used to share a taxi with him and had first met him when I showed him around the school the previous year. He was always singing at break and lunchtime, and also in lessons as many of his year group kept telling me. He started a club called "Grotto Club" which I was a member of and later I was the "merchandise man". We used to have meetings once a week in the exam room and had about six members. The club went on for about two years, and we produced a song, newsletters, a mascot and even a website. Later my friend became the head of other clubs such as Terraria (a computer game) club and a computer club which I sometimes used to go to. One boy who wanted to join the Grotto Club was in my year, and in the taxi I told my friend not to let him join because the only reason he wanted to join was so he could bully me. He and another boy were constantly annoying me and when I was playing football kept saying that I was no good and tackling me even if we were on the same team. Some of my other friends said that they were bothering them as well.

Whilst I was in Year 10, we had one particular science teacher who was like a little dictator. As soon as someone in the class started talking, even if it was about the work, she would get her stopwatch out and start timing us. She would then only stop it if the room was silent. At the end of the lesson she would double the time on her watch and make us all stay in after class for that much longer. This was despite the fact that 90% of the class had not spoken at all. She had done this about two or three times in this one particular lesson and I decided that I could take it no longer. Why should I miss my break if I had done nothing wrong? I stood up and walked out the room. The teacher said, "Where are you going?" to which I replied, "Thank you for the lesson. I am going for lunch." When she saw me during lunchtime, she went absolutely mad at me. To be honest, I just stood there and took it. I was so depressed at the time that I could not be bothered getting wound up about this. In another science class I always used to sit by a friend of mine and we both found the lessons exceedingly boring. We devised a game where we would each take it in turns to write BCFC or AVFC, the initials of the football teams we supported, on a piece of paper and the other person had to find it. It was actually very fun and made the lessons seem shorter.

In my opinion some teachers used to speak to pupils in a derogatory manner. Normally it was not me they were speaking to but others in my class, but this still used to annoy me because it was just unfair that they could speak to us like this. A lot of the anger that I used to feel towards the teachers would all come out when I got home and would be directed towards my parents. I would always tell them that I felt like saying certain things. I never did say these things because I did not want to get into trouble. They had a few posters around the school saying things such as: "You are the master of your own destiny," and things like that. When I saw them, I used to want to rip them off the wall because they were not true. If we were the masters of our own destiny, then why were we being forced to attend school and do lessons that we found boring?

Every morning before I got in the taxi, I would often be fighting with my school tie. I used to see the tie as something that represented the school and I would always try and hide it or go without it. Sometimes I would just throw it on the floor outside my house, and then my mum would have to give it to the taxi driver. My teacher who used to teach the small group suggested that I left one of my ties at school in case I ever came in without one or I was in a "tieless" situation, as she used to say.

Most people probably don't like doing exams, but I actually quite enjoy them. When I was doing my GCSEs a lot of our lessons were spent doing past papers. Doing these past papers was actually more enjoyable and relaxing than listening to lectures from the teachers or having to copy page after page of notes. In our study skills lessons my friend and I would just work our way through all of the past papers. I did not do my exams in the exam room with the rest of the year. Instead, I did my exams in a room on my own with one teacher. I was also allowed extra time for my exams. My friend and I had our last GCSE exams on the same day. His last exam was in the morning and my last exam was in the afternoon. To celebrate at lunchtime, we both went outside and sang some CBeebies songs. He sang the hello song and I sang the goodbye song from the CBeebies show *Something Special*.

"Accept responsibility for your life. Know that it is you who will get you where you want to go, no one else."

Les Brown

CHAPTER 12
The new Headteacher

"Autistic pupils are three times as likely to be excluded from school as pupils with no special educational needs (SEN)."

National Autistic Society, New teachers' resources to avoid excluding autistic pupils

During my final few years at secondary school we had a new headteacher and my school life changed for the worse. A lot of changes were introduced, new rules imposed and timetables altered, which for me were very difficult to adapt to. I felt that a lot of the good strategies that had been put in place for me and other students like me were being destroyed.

When the Headteacher first arrived at the school I actually quite liked him, but after experiencing the effect he had on my school life I changed my opinion and began to really dislike him. It may well have been that the Headteacher was doing what he thought was best for the school, and possibly even for me. However, a lot of the changes he introduced had a huge negative impact on me. I also feel, and my dad does, that he was inflexible in his approach, which meant that some compromises which would have lessened the impact of the wider changes on me, and made my life a lot less stressful, were not made.

When I started, the school had a wonderful SENCO. She really understood the problems that I was having and throughout my time at the school helped me and my family enormously. She was also a great point of contact for my parents, who both said she was not just understanding but always took action to improve things. Apart from my LSA (Learning Support Assistant) she was also one of the only teachers that I could trust, and if I ever had any worries, I knew that I could go and speak to her. Soon after the new Headteacher arrived she left, and the school never again, whilst I was there, had another SENCO anywhere near as good as she was.

One incident that I'll never forget was when a teacher found a dirty cup in his classroom. The Headteacher, assuming one of my class was responsible, made the whole class stand up in assembly (in my opinion to embarrass and make an example of us). This was despite the fact that I had done nothing wrong, which I am pretty sure they would have known. It was excruciatingly painful to see my friends (many with special needs), some of whom were extremely shy, having to endure this ordeal that was totally unnecessary. The Headteacher went up to each person saying, "Was it you who did this?" to which we had to reply, "No Sir." One of my friends just said "No" instead of "No Sir," so he was shouted at again. After the incident another teacher came up to me to apologise, and said that if she had known this was going to happen, she would not have allowed it to. My dad called the school to complain and the teacher apologised to him also. I was just annoyed, but I know it traumatised some of my friends. I felt like the Headteacher would not acknowledge that Asperger's was a real thing, and I believe he thought that we were just naughty and would not allow any individual to have their own rule. For instance, my dad called the school to explain how much the change to the timetable had caused me stress and in particular the extended extra time put on at the end of each Friday. My dad suggested that I should be allowed to leave early on a Friday because of the stress I was suffering and that it could be written into my Statement. The answer was no! My dad told me that he believed it was the Headteacher's inflexibility of thought and determination to not let people be different that prevented this.

One of the options that I took for my GCSEs was called "study skills". It meant that instead of doing a certain subject you had free time to do homework for other subjects. It also meant that I did not have to bring so much work home with me.

It was like a lifeline for me and sometimes I would get all of my homework completed in those lessons. However, the new Headteacher decided that these lessons should be changed by adding set work to make it more of a subject. I got really stressed about this as this is something that I had not signed up for and I was worried about not being able to get all of my work done. It transpired that whilst some of my friends had to do the set work within part of these lessons, I was still able to use the lessons solely to do my homework.

Another thing that this Headteacher changed was the form groups which we had to register in every morning and afternoon. Up until this point I had been in the same form with the same people from my year for four years. However, they changed all the forms around so that the forms became a mixture of different year groups. I really did not like this and was very stressed about this change. For a start, I had a few friends in my form who I would talk to every morning and it would settle me in for the day. When the new forms were announced I suddenly went from having about four friends to only one in my form. My teaching assistant said that if I wanted to, I could move to another form group where three of my friends were. I wanted to move to this form, but then my friend in my current form would have been left on his own. This was a huge change to deal with for me and I don't think I ever really got over it.

In 2012, as a consequence of the increased stress I was suffering from due to all these changes, my dad had a conversation with the Headteacher to explain the many issues I had with all the changes introduced. The Headteacher did not appreciate my dad explaining to him why all these changes were so difficult for someone like me with Asperger's to cope with. As a result of this conversation, the Headteacher sent an email to the council which he concluded by saying: "As provider of Alex's Statement you must decide where the needs described in his Statement can now be met as it is clear his family feel [the school] led by myself is damaging Alex's mental health."

Incidentally, I only found out about this once I had left school and started reading through all of my dad's emails and notes.

Consequently, my dad was banned from holding my Annual Review meeting at the school. After taking advice from the National Autistic Society (NAS), the children's charity Coram and the Equality Advice Service, my dad contacted the council as he believed that the school had infringed my rights under the Equality Act 2010 and that the Local Education Authority (LEA) was in breach of law concerning the long delay for my Annual Review meeting to take place. The Headteacher had banned my dad from going to the school for the overdue Annual Review meeting; hence it was arranged off site. The council advised that it was best that my dad did not attend in case he antagonised the Headteacher! The council promised my parents that they would be supportive in the meeting and would not let the Headteacher overpower it. However, the council representative did very little in the meeting and my mum said that nothing was achieved. In fact, the council's advice was to not upset the Headteacher and to try and take a conciliatory approach. Indeed, the Headteacher concluded that "school rules are not going to change" and closed the review, stating nothing in my Statement needed changing! My dad was very annoyed with the council because of the lack of support they provided and the subsequent consequences to me of no changes being made and wrote an email to them documenting the whole thing.

When Ofsted investigated the school, they provided parents the opportunity to anonymously complain. However, they reserved the right to publish the anonymous complaints. Therefore, my dad could not share our experience because if he had it would have been obvious who it was and that could have risked me being kicked out of the school!

At this time, the charity that I am involved with even set up a meeting with a number of parents from my school that were also having problems with the school. My dad tells me that some of the stories they were relaying were quite alarming. It just shows how one change in a school can affect so many people. I was so miserable when I was doing my

GCSEs that I considered not going to the sixth form, but in the end, there was nowhere else suitable for me to go.

"The ultimate measure of a man is not where he stands in moments of comfort and convenience, but where he stands at times of challenge and controversy."

Martin Luther King Jr

CHAPTER 13
The problems with schools

"Fewer than 5 in 10 teachers say that they are confident about supporting a child on the autism spectrum."

National Autistic Society,
Autism and Education in England 2017

There are a number of problems with schools when it comes to looking after people with autism and Asperger's and I have a number of suggestions of what can be done to help resolve some of these problems.

Small allowances can make a huge difference

A friend of mine took history for his GCSEs and he soon found out that he hated the subject. He used to go around the school every day telling everyone who he met that history was boring as well as leaving "history is boring" notes all around the school. He also used to write it on the whiteboards and made his own history is boring song. Why was it that the school could not let him drop this subject? At the end of the day, it would have made him a lot happier and less stressed. I'm sure it would have benefited his family as well as the teacher. She must have been sick and tired of hearing him saying her lesson was boring. Such a small change would have benefited a lot of people.

A lot of the time it is very small changes that make the most amount of difference. They won't affect anyone else, but they will make a huge difference to that individual's life. One of the big problems at school for me was wearing the uniform. If the school had allowed me to wear my own clothes, then I would have been so much happier and less stressed each and every day. Plus, nobody else would have been affected by it. In fact, by not allowing these small changes to happen it can often result in more work and effort for the teachers. For example, the teachers would not have had to keep pulling me up for wearing my own jumpers and sports kit. They would not have had to deal with my parents calling up and they would not have had to deal with the knock-on effects of the stress that wearing the uniform caused me. It would have been easier for everyone if they had let me wear my own clothes. Some teachers are reluctant because they say, "Well, if he wears his own clothes, then everyone else will want to." But they were already letting me do things that others could not do like having "time outs", so therefore how was this any different? I felt as if they were making allowances as and when it suited them.

Another change that could have been made is one that allowed me to have an extra day off school. Sometimes a five-day week was too stressful and having one less day at school would have made the week easier to cope with. The SENCO at my secondary school even suggested that I should have Fridays off. Saturdays were my favourite day of the week as I was not at school and still had Sunday to look forward to. However, Sundays were not as great as I would spend most of the day worrying about school on the Monday. It felt like I only had a one-day weekend!

A little knowledge is dangerous

Many of the teachers that I came across had preconceived ideas about what autism and Asperger's were. This was especially apparent at my primary school. Many of them thought that they were experts on the subject when in actual fact they knew very little. Sometimes I feel it is the teachers that know a lot about autism that confess not to know much or who want to learn more. However, it is the teachers who do not know much that pretend to know a lot. Also, I believe many teachers refuse to accept we have it and are not willing to treat us any differently or to change the rules to help us and relieve our stresses. Because they can't see a problem, as it's a hidden disability, they think that there is not one. They think that because everyone else copes ok then so should we. Therefore, there needs to be more awareness of autism and Asperger's in schools, possibly via teacher training days. In addition, there needs to be a system where people with autism are only put into a teacher's care if the teacher has received this training.

Independent schools should adhere to the same jurisdiction as state schools

One thing my dad felt was a major obstacle preventing me from getting the real help I needed was that private independent schools didn't have to adhere to the same rules as state schools. As my secondary school was a private independent school, then when it came to the problems we were experiencing, the council said that they were not able to do anything. If, however, it had been a state school, then the council could have intervened and been able to exert influence to bring about appropriate changes. With the council sending so many people to the school who had Asperger's, it was incredible to think that they could not exert some influence. My dad believes a solution to this issue is that councils should only be allowed to send children with autism and Asperger's to schools that adhere to council rules. There should be parity between state schools and private schools.

Small schools are preferable

From my own experience, private schools are often smaller than mainstream schools, which for us can be a hugely positive thing. Mainstream schools are often too big and stressful for people with Asperger's. There can be too many people, too much noise and too much going on for us to cope with. Even if there are no suitable schools within our area for us to go to, then the smaller the school the better we will cope. Secondary school can be harder for us to navigate than primary school because they are often much bigger. In primary school we normally have one teacher and one classroom, but in secondary school we have multiple teachers and multiple classrooms. The amount of changes that we have to cope with is also a huge factor. Plus, as we are often different to your average neurotypical individual (someone who does not have autism) then we are more likely to be bullied. I know if I had gone to a mainstream school, then the bright and colourful clothes that I wear as well as my interest in children's TV may have attracted unwanted attention from other students. Luckily, at my secondary school I was never bullied for these reasons.

A tailored approach can reap rewards

Every lesson we were given exercise books full of boring white paper to write on. I always wanted colourful paper as it would have made the lessons less monotonous and boring. Whilst I was at primary school my grandad had bought me some Letts Little Wizard's maths activity books. I really enjoyed doing these because although I was still doing maths, which at school I found boring, the pages were all very colourful with pictures of wizards and witches. Plus, all of the questions were wizard-based. Whilst I still refused to do my school homework, I would willingly do these activity books. He also managed to find me some football activity maths books which I also enjoyed. If the teachers had centred the work on my specialist interest, which is football, then that would have also made the lessons less boring. For example, in maths if instead of asking me what the area of the rectangle was, the teacher had asked me what the area of the Birmingham City football pitch was, then I would have been more engaged with the subject. This is why it is so important that teachers who teach students with Asperger's truly understand the condition.

Minimise surprises!

In school there are many unknowns, which people with Asperger's can find very difficult. The unknowns range from who will be at school in the morning to what we will be learning in each lesson. Even situations that to most people seem the same can be hard for us to cope with as there will be many variations of the everyday normalities. For example, you get the same bus to school every day, from the same bus stop that goes on the same route. However, we will be worried because the driver may be different, the people we sit next to may be different or it may be a different type of bus to the one we usually get. In lessons the uncertainty of whether or not we would have homework used to make me a nervous wreck. It would have been far easier to have known of any homework at the start of the lesson. That way I could have focused on the lesson.

Specialist schools

A lot of my teachers at my secondary school were excellent and it's a shame that they could not all get together with similar teachers from other schools to set up a special school for people with Asperger's in Birmingham, a school where all of the teachers had experience of teaching Asperger's students and genuinely enjoyed the challenges that it presents. I know it would have been a wonderful school and helped so many people. For a start, all the pupils would have had their own set of unique rules that would have helped them cope throughout the day. Even if one specific school in the area had a section set up within it that helped us, then that would be a great start and a place that parents could know their children are being looked after.

Treat us as individuals

My dad told me that in business, looking after employees equates to higher productivity. All employees are different, so rather than one rule for all, where possible it is wise to accommodate their individual preferences and often it's only minor things e.g. a different chair, seat by the window, free hot drinks etc. This will make the employees happier and work more effectively. He says it's the same with Asperger's students. Often, it's only small changes that are required to accommodate their idiosyncrasies, which would mean they are happier and less stressed, the teachers have less to do and the family have an easier life. Everybody wins!

"Life isn't about waiting for the storm to pass; it's about learning to dance in the rain."

Vivian Greene

CHAPTER 14
English lessons

"Reading comprehension involves the ability to actively construct meaning from print. Reading comprehension can be a challenge for many children with autism spectrum disorders, as these children have been shown to have difficulty integrating language and social messages and interpreting emotions and emotional intent."

Cynthia Merrifield, St John Fisher College,
Enhancing reading comprehension for
students with autism

When I first started secondary school, we always had to have a reading book with us to read during some of our English lessons. Whilst I enjoyed reading, I only really enjoyed reading non-fiction books, especially footballers' autobiographies. Our teacher always used to try and make me read fiction books, but I never wanted to and always went back to my non-fiction books. If I was reading a non-fiction book, I felt as though I was learning stuff, but when I was reading a fiction book I felt like I was wasting my time; after all, it's just "make believe"! I had felt like this at primary school too and could not stand the reading books that we had to read in class. I remember that I told my mum that if I had told her to read a footballer's autobiography and she was not interested in it then I would let her read something else. I did not see the point in reading a book that you were not interested in. This logical or "black and white" approach is very common with Asperger's and I think it's one reason why it would help for Asperger's students to study at a specialist school.

Before I started GCSEs at secondary school, English was my worst subject as I hated reading fiction books, found Shakespeare boring and did not understand idioms etc. To be honest, I thought that the whole subject was boring and did not like the teachers as I felt that they were too strict. But as soon as I started GCSEs I had a new English teacher who was the best teacher that I ever had, and as a result, English suddenly went from being my worst subject to my favourite subject! If I was stressed, he would allow me to read my football programmes or listen to music, so when it came to doing the work, I was much more relaxed and willing to do it. Because he had been so understanding and supportive towards me, I wanted to return the favour and to complete his work to the best of my abilities. He also used to wear bright-coloured clothes, which always made me happy, and he did not mind if I had not done the homework. It transpired that I achieved my best GCSE grade in this subject!

Before I started GCSEs, my dad expected me to get a D in English. In hindsight, I must have been subconsciously sabotaging my grades just to get back at the teachers. It just shows that sometimes it is the teacher who makes the biggest difference and also how important it is to work with an Asperger's child rather than against them. If pupils enjoy the lesson, then they are more likely to absorb the teaching and obtain higher grades than they are expecting. However, if they do not enjoy the lesson, then they are more likely to ignore the teaching and get worse grades than they are expecting because they will not be motivated. The teacher I had before I started my GCSEs would not let me read my football programmes, which used to relieve my stresses, and so I just became even more stressed. Then when it came to the work my brain had just shut down and I could not be bothered to do it because I was too stressed.

English can be one of the hardest subjects for someone who has Asperger's. I know a lot of my friends struggled with it at school. Subjects like maths are very clear as the answers will either be right or wrong, but with English there are infinite possible answers to a question. There were about 50 people in my year at secondary school and for the same piece of work everyone will have written something completely different. The teachers will then have to interpret the grades from what we have written, and different teachers will often have different interpretation and thus give different results. As it is not a "black and white", "right or wrong" subject, it can be harder for us to understand. Whilst I am good at English, I still don't understand or see the point in some of the language we have to use. I mean, a strawberry is a strawberry. Why do you have to go and give it human feelings and emotions?

Sometimes sentences or pieces of writing had hidden meanings and I found it really hard to work out what they were as I could just not see them. For example, if somebody had written "The dog was black," to me it was because the dog was actually the colour black and nothing to do with indicating depression or any other feeling or emotion. Also, there are loads of idioms and phrases that we had to either write or talk about which to me don't make any sense. Abstract themes in certain books and pieces of writing were often being missed because if they were not spelt out then how was I supposed to know what they were?

"There are no limits. There are plateaus, but you must not stay there, you must go beyond them."

Bruce Lee

CHAPTER 15
Changes

"The world can seem a very unpredictable and confusing place to autistic people, who often prefer to have a daily routine so that they know what is going to happen every day. They may want to always travel the same way to and from school or work, or eat exactly the same food for breakfast."

National Autistic Society,
Obsessions, repetitive behaviour and routines

When I was at school there were a lot of changes. At the time they seemed daunting to me as I did not know what was happening and it felt as though my whole way of living was being turned upside down. One of the options I chose for GCSE was P.E. and in my final year I must have had about two or three practical lessons each week. But although I had so many P.E. lessons, I only wore the school kit once, choosing instead to wear my own football kits from home. It was not because I was deliberately trying to be naughty but it was my way of bending the rules slightly to relieve my stress and give myself a little bit of freedom. I was having a terrible time at school and the uniform was one of my longstanding issues. If I am wearing colourful clothes, then I can conquer anything. However, if I am wearing dark-coloured clothes, then I feel as though I am hiding my personality and can feel depressed. In the end, the school told me that as long as I wore the school colours, I could wear my own kit. So, every week I just wore my Birmingham City kit and it definitely made me feel less stressed. Such a small change made a whole lot of difference to me, which is why I can never understand why society makes someone feel so stressed by insisting that they wear a uniform. It seems it is ingrained in society that people are not allowed to be different!

I also used to wear my own colourful jumpers into school. Again, I was not trying to be naughty and deliberately break the rules but I was trying to make myself feel better and more comfortable. My teaching assistant was always telling me that I was not allowed to wear them, but I did not really take any notice of her. She would often take my jumpers off me and only allow me to wear them during breaks and lunchtime. I told my mum that I would superglue one of my jumpers to my school shirt so that I would feel more like my true self and so that nobody could make me take it off. It was also suggested that I wear a colourful shirt underneath my school shirt. This would have actually made me feel worse as I would have felt like I was being forced to hide my personality. In the end, they allowed me to wear my own jumper as long as it was red, the colour of the old school jumpers. Wearing my own jumper into school felt like I was bringing some of my brilliant home life with me, which made me feel less stressed.

During this year the Headteacher added an extra lesson at the end of every Friday without seemingly any consideration for how this would affect me and others who had Asperger's. We used to finish at 3:10, but with the added lesson we now finished at 4:00. I could not cope with this change. My mental health was badly affected because I was so stressed and my GCSEs were nearly ruined. The extended lesson was P.E. and so I would always wear what I liked as in my opinion it was my own time anyway. I was so depressed at the time because of the changes the Headteacher had introduced that my parents were considering pulling me out of the school because I was so upset. After having a talk with my Learning Support Assistant about half way through Year 11, I decided that I was not going to let one person, even if unintentionally, ruin my grades, because once I had left the school, I would never have to see him again. Every time I had negative thoughts my dad would always say to me that I had "stinkin' thinkin'" and needed to be positive. He would say, "Remember the advice you were given that you have the intelligence to solve this problem yourself." So, taking his advice I decided to look at the bigger picture and this approach helped me to cope.

After the new Headteacher arrived, the school timetable would change every year. Just when I would get used to the new timetable it would change again and I would be back to square one. Everything about the timetables would change, the length of the lessons, how long we had for break and lunch etc. Having rigid timetables are really helpful for people with Asperger's as we then know exactly what is happening and when, and they give us a sense of stability and routine. However, the number of timetable changes that were enforced during my GCSE years made me very stressed and made me feel vulnerable. I consequently had no routine and no sense of stability, which I desperately needed.

It used to also annoy me how the sixth formers could wear what they liked but still chose to wear the school uniform or what I would call the school uniform i.e. black trousers and a white shirt. I was forced to wear it, and if I had been given the choice, I would have worn my own colourful clothes. I used to think that we should be the ones allowed to wear what we like and they should be the ones who should have to wear the school uniform. When I was younger, I used to think that people who chose to wear black or grey had no personality and had given up on life. Sometimes I would say things to family members that may not have been that nice. I was not trying to hurt anybody's feelings but that is how much I hated having to wear those colours. I could not understand how anybody else could like wearing black or grey. Dark clothes used to make me think about school, which was not somewhere that I liked to go. I still hate wearing those colours to this day, but my opinion now is that everyone is different and can choose to wear what they like. I suppose I have just accepted that some people like these colours. My mum recently bought a black-coloured car with black interior and I have nicknamed it the "death mobile".

I know for certain that my love of bright colours has had a positive impact on my family. My Grandad Doug was one person who always used to wear black trousers. Every time he played golf, he would always wear a pair of black trousers. Now he has three pairs of pink trousers which he wears for golf. I honestly can't remember the last time he wore black trousers. I also bought him a multi-coloured flowery shirt which matches the one that I have. If we go out for a meal, we often both put them on together. My grandad even told me that wearing these bright colours actually made him feel happier. My mum and grandma also have one of these flowery shirts, although they don't wear them as often as my grandad and I!

Recently my dad decided that we would be having some work done on the house and building an extension out the back. As we were having an extension to the ground floor, it was decided that we would also have an extension to the upper floor as well. This meant that my bedroom would be extended and that my whole family would be moving rooms. Even now I still don't believe that this is going to happen, even though I have seen architects in the house and all of my dad's paperwork. One night when I went to bed I started to think about where I would put everything in my new room and I just could not get to sleep. I realised that because I have a lot of belongings, some of my possessions may not fit into my new room. I started to have a bit of a panic attack and it took me ages to get to sleep that evening.

I have a love of routine, and when I was younger, I used to have to know exactly what we were doing, when and how long for so I could feel relaxed and not become worried or anxious. Now I have become an adult, I still have a love of routine and order and it has got to the extent where everything in my bedroom has an exact place. I can tell if somebody has moved even the smallest of items, such as a pencil, or has slightly ruffled my duvet. I can tell you where everything is in my room down to the last paperclip. My wardrobe is arranged in colour order and everything in my drawers is positioned in the same direction. It is well documented that people with Asperger's like to have everything to be kept the same so that we can feel secure. Even if the slightest thing changes, then we can start to wobble; this is why we need to be told of any changes in advance. Just think about all the changes that are made when you start a new school year. Well, to us it can feel like we are starting a whole new school again!

"Try and look at the positives in every situation and don't let your 'stinkin' thinkin" get in the way."

Andrew Manners

CHAPTER 16
Sensory overload

"People with autism are often highly sensitive to their environments. That, of course, means different things to different people on the spectrum – but in general people with autism have unusually sensitive 'sensory' systems, meaning that their senses sight, hearing, touch, smell, and taste can all be easily overloaded."

Verywell Health, Autism and sensory overload

Everyone who has Asperger's is different, so what I find helpful may be the thing that someone else struggles with. To autistic people the world can seem a terrifying place. It can feel like there is too much noise, too many people or just simply too much information for our brains to cope with all at once. We are often over- or under-sensitive to many sensory issues. These can be sounds, smells, sight such as eye contact and light, the way objects feel or certain foods taste. Sometimes going out in public to places like shopping centres and zoos can make us really stressed due to the number of things that we can hear and see. If you ever see a child in a shop or a supermarket who is crying or shouting at their parents, then just think for a moment. They may not just be naughty; they may have autism!

I am constantly thinking of things that neurotypical individuals (people who do not have autism) would never come up with. They may be strange, obscure and at times seem as though I am just being deliberately silly, but they make perfect sense to me. They are all logical questions that I am intrigued to find out the answers to. As I am passionate about football, I am often talking about it with my family. I was in the car with my grandad a few months ago and we were talking about the Premier League. As you may know, if two teams finish on the same number of points then the team with a better goal difference finishes in a higher position. I asked my grandad what would happen if every team in the league finished on the same points and every other stat i.e. goal difference, number of cards etc. was exactly the same as well. I don't think he knew what to say because he thought it was a stupid question, because to him that would never happen and would be impossible. But in reality, whilst very unlikely it is not impossible.

I am very inquisitive and I am always wondering what if this happened or what if they did that, hence the reason why I ask so many "what if" questions. I also always wonder about how certain things were invented and how they got their name, like "Who first called a chair a chair?" or "How did someone first invent the drinks coaster?" Sometimes when I am looking at objects, a world of thoughts and possibilities come into my mind. Take the drinks coaster. I'm not just merely looking at it and dismissing it but instead my mind is in a whirl. "Why is it called a coaster?", "Who invented it?", "Was it invented for the purpose we use it for?" and "What event occurred for someone to realise they needed something like this?" are just some of the things that would be going through my mind. This is the same for most objects that I look at.

Whilst it's not true for everybody who has Asperger's, it's quite a common perception that people with Asperger's don't like noise. Even everyday noises like hand dryers or the sound of somebody making a cup of tea can be overwhelming to us. For a non-autistic person, they may not notice the sounds that are going on around them in everyday life. But if you took just one minute to sit back and listen, then you will be surprised by the amount of different noises that you will be able to hear. Now imagine all of those noises were ten times as loud and that is how they might sound to us. Some people may say, "Well, can't you just focus on something else and it will stop you thinking about the noise." Whilst this may work for a lot of people, it does not actually mean that the noise has stopped and so we will still be able to hear it. Repetitive noises like a car alarm can be the most annoying sounds to us as they seem never-ending.

One sound that has always irritated me is the sound of a ticking radiator and it is torture. My parents could never understand how such a small noise could be such an issue. However, for me it was like someone was right next to my ear banging on a drum as loudly as they could, non-stop. Night after night I would trudge downstairs to ask if the radiator could be turned off, always to my parent's moans. I know in some American prisons they keep prisoners in cells with nothing more than a drip, drip, drip of a tap. It is a form of torture and night after night this is what it felt like to me. I don't like the heat anyway, so to me the radiator in my bedroom was just a big lump of useless metal that served no purpose other than to keep me awake at night!

The clicking of nails, the sniffing of someone who has a cold or the scratching of metal are three sounds that just go straight through me. I can tolerate some noises for a certain length of time, but for other noises, as soon as I hear them then it has already gone on for too long. Every noise for many people with Asperger's sounds as though it is being amplified through speakers. (Imagine how if you are at a disco with loud music then after a while your ears may start to hurt.)

As well as certain noises, the feel of certain objects can also really irritate me, such as socks and t-shirts. I don't have a problem wearing these items, but it's the little added extras that really don't need to be included that annoy me, like the cotton labels in the back of many shirts. I find them really itchy and irritating and, in my opinion, unnecessary. For me, having one of these labels in the back of my shirt feels as though there is a big, jagged rock going up and down my neck. I have always taken my labels out of shirts, and when it came to passing on my clothes to my younger cousins, well they had no idea what any of the sizes were! Many of the football shirts that I own have labels that are just like stickers that you can't feel. I wish all manufacturers would use these instead of the thick, itchy cotton ones that they have become so accustomed to putting in the back of our shirts.

The seams at the end of socks are another example of something that feels horrible. I usually buy seamless socks, but sometimes my grandma has to cut the end of the socks off and sew them back on, inside out. This is so that I won't be able to feel the seams. They feel just like a piece of wire scratching your toes. At school I hated the feeling of clay and I could not bear to touch it. Once, I even got told off for flicking a small piece of clay under the table because I could not bear to pick it up and touch it. This is one of the reasons why ceramics was one of my worst subjects. I also hated doing my top button up because it felt like I was being strangled. Tucking my shirt in also felt uncomfortable, so I only ever used to tuck the front of my shirt in because this was the only part the teachers could see.

Problems with the sense of touch can not only come from objects but also from people. People with Asperger's may not feel very comfortable with physical interaction, like if we are given a hug or a pat on the back. I know I don't like it when someone gives me a pat on the back. People with Asperger's tend to like their own personal space, more so than non-autistic people. Whilst I love to give my mum a hug every now and then, I still don't like giving others one, even other people within my family. I think with my mum it's a sense of comfort as I know exactly how a hug from her feels.

"Successful people are 100% convinced that they are masters of their own destiny. They're not creatures of circumstance. They create circumstance. If the circumstances around them suck, they change them."

Jordan Belfort

CHAPTER 17
Communication and phrases

"Individuals with high-functioning autism can have very high IQs, but they nevertheless struggle with communicating with others, may often be preoccupied with small details or the structure of things, and have difficulty 'reading' another person's emotions or facial expressions. Children with high-functioning autism also have a hard time understanding idioms, even though their basic language skills may be highly advanced."

MedicalXpress,
How people with autism spectrum disorders understand idioms and other figures of speech

Communication is an area where I believe that my Asperger's has really benefited me. Whilst a lot of people with Asperger's find it difficult to hold a conversation, I find it very easy. When I used to go on holiday, I would always rather have gone shopping with my grandma than go to the beach with my cousins. I was always good at talking to grown-ups and I could not see why we as children were treated so differently to them. There was one restaurant that we used to go past whilst on holiday where it was adults only. For me, this really used to get me annoyed as I felt a sense of injustice. I knew that I was never going to go there, but it was just unfair. To a person like me who used to eat all the same things as an adult, behave in the same way as an adult and talk in the same way as an adult, I could not see how I was any different and why I should not be allowed in the restaurant. Whilst in many ways I acted older than my age, I still liked many childish things that at the time would have been considered too young for me. For example, I still like watching many children's TV shows.

But, for many people with Asperger's this is not the case, and they struggle to hold conversations, struggle to look people in the eye and struggle to process language. To look someone in the eye can feel as though their eyes are burning or someone is poking their eyes out with a pin. Sometimes people with Asperger's will lose eye contact so they can focus on the conversation. Speaking to someone new can be especially daunting as they are left open to all possibilities and don't have a clue of what to expect. My dad told me how he always found it strange that when my friends came round, they would not speak to him or look him in the eye. However, as soon as he left, they would talk, laugh and joke with me as if they were fine. It was almost as if my dad spoke in a different language that they did not understand. To him it could have felt as though I had waved a magic wand over them. Although we all had Asperger's, we were all completely different, but we did not notice each other's idiosyncrasies. When we are together, we accept each other for who we are, unlike neurotypical individuals who tend to constantly judge people. I think it is all about trust. When an autistic person trusts you then they are more comfortable and can be more open towards you.

When somebody is speaking to someone with Asperger's, whatever they might be saying, it can feel as though there is a whirlwind going on inside our brain. It is like we are sifting through hundreds of websites trying to find the best answer to their question. Even though I am very good at communicating with others, I still experience these feelings and still find having a conversation a little difficult at times. I don't have a problem with eye contact, but sometimes I struggle to know how long I should keep eye contact for. I subconsciously know that after about ten seconds I should look away for a few seconds before regaining eye contact. Also, if I am talking with a large crowd of people, especially about a subject that I'm not too familiar with, I'm not always sure when to say something or even what to say. A lot of the time we think of things that non-autistic people can't get their head around. We may even think of something completely unrelated to the subject everyone else is talking about. You could say that small talk is often difficult for people with Asperger's. I could talk for hours about football grounds, but when it comes to the small talk, e.g. "nice weather", I just don't see the point.

Open-ended questions can also be really challenging. I told my grandad that I was working on Monday, Tuesday and Wednesday, and he came back with "Where?" I sat there blank for a few seconds before telling him that I did not understand his question. I know that he was only asking me where I was working, but was he asking me where I was working Monday, where I was working Tuesday or where I was working on Wednesday? A lot of people may think that I was just being a little awkward, but I really didn't understand the question. So many answers to the question were going through my mind that I became so overloaded with information that I just couldn't scramble an answer together!

Phrases and sayings like "hit the hay" or "raining cats and dogs" can really leave us confused. Instead of saying, "I'm going to hit the hay," would it not be easier to just say, "I'm going to bed." Some of us might think that you are actually going to go and hit a barrel of hay. After all, it takes fewer words to say it and at least everyone will understand you. In my opinion, if someone is going to say these types of phrases that to me don't make any sense, then they might as well be talking in a different language. When I was in secondary school, I had a lot of speech and language lessons where we talked about what different idioms and phrases meant. Whilst I now know what a lot of them mean, I still don't see the point in using them. It would have saved me a lot of time at school if people just used plain old English to say what they mean.

I take what people say very literally. This could really affect some people with Asperger's, especially if they were meant to do something important. When we were answering questions in school, I learnt that the correct answer did not always give you the mark and what you had to put down was the "expected answer". One of the common questions in maths exams was "Find x." Well, the correct answer would have been to circle the letter x. However, the expected answer was to work out the value of x. Why they could not ask you this is beyond me!

When my grandad and I play golf, he will often say to me, "You didn't hit that," if I have hit a bad shot. I always reply, "Well, how did the ball move and go over there if I did not hit it?" Before we have dinner, he likes me or my grandma to lay the table with mats, cutlery, salt and pepper etc. One evening he asked me to lay the table but instead of saying, "Can you lay the table?" he said, "Can you lay the knives and forks?" When I did lay the knives and forks, he said, "You have not finished, what about the other things?" I did think about the other items but thought that he must only want knives and forks, and so I did exactly what he asked. On holiday my dad told me to boil the kettle. I did this and then went and sat back down. After a few minutes he said, "Aren't you going to make me a cup of tea?" I would have happily made him a cup of tea, but he did not ask me to make him one.

One story that I heard was from a lady who had said to her son, "Can you lay the table?" He replied to her saying yes, but when she had come back about 15 minutes later the table had not been laid. She asked him why it was not laid, and he told his mum that she had not asked him to lay it. You see she did not say, "Will you lay the table?" She had only said, "Can you lay the table?" and yes, he can physically lay the table.

Once when I was in the supermarket and I was at the checkout with my grandma we had an incident with a cucumber. I picked it up and said to her, "What does this remind you of?" At home I had a green baseball bat and that is what the cucumber reminded me of. She told me to be quiet and afterwards said that it was a very rude thing to say. She even told me how the lady on the checkout had given us a weird look, which I must not have noticed. I asked her why it was rude because a baseball bat is not a rude thing to talk about. She thought I had meant that the cucumber looked like a part of a man's body. However, this had not even crossed my mind. For a start, it was green and a man's body parts are not green, and secondly it was too long to be a man's body part!

"Good things come to those who wait … greater things come to those who get off their ass and do anything to make it happen."

Unknown

CHAPTER 18
Family Equip

The National Autistic Society has over 23,000 members, making it the UK's largest charity for autistic people and their families. However, there are many other autism and Asperger's charities all over the UK, like Family Equip.

Family Equip is a small charity in Solihull that was set up in 2004 to help children and young adults who have difficulties such as Asperger's syndrome. When I was eleven, I started attending the charity's therapeutic clubs that ran one evening a week. The clubs allowed me to meet other people who were going through the same challenges that I was, as well as being somewhere where I could just be myself. As well as having discussions on a number of different topics, from belonging to responsibility, we were able to join in a host of other activities, including table tennis and PlayStation. When I was about seventeen, I went from being a member at these clubs to becoming a volunteer, something that I still do to this day, helping at the older boys and younger boys clubs on a Monday evening.

The clubs had been set up to enable the youngsters to gain a better understanding of themselves, build self-esteem and social skills, and to help them become more independent. At these therapeutic clubs we always used to have discussions on different topics, as I have mentioned above. They would often give us a piece of paper with what was called a blob picture on. This was a series of blob men all doing different things and we had to pick the one that best described how we were feeling at that time or that we thought had certain emotions. We also had a series of cards with different pictures on of people in different situations and would have to describe how we thought the people in the pictures were feeling. We also used to do group activities like scavenger hunts or circle games where we would have to remember what other people had said or the action they had done.

Family Equip has helped me and my family tremendously over the years. For a start, they were instrumental in helping me to get my Statement and advised us on whom we should speak to at the time. They also advised us on which secondary school I should go to and helped me to get into my secondary school. When my dad and a lot of other parents had issues with the school during my GCSE years the charity set up a meeting with the parents who were having problems. The charity's founder tried to resolve the issues by talking to the school but met with some resistance. At least the charity was willing to help. For a short while my mum also volunteered and helped at some of the charity's therapeutic clubs for girls and siblings that ran on Tuesday evenings.

In 2012, I helped to organise a charity football match with my Uncle Tim to raise some money for Family Equip. It was a great event and I had the job of putting together the match programme. All in all, the event raised over £500 for the charity. Then in 2017, I started a crowdfunding campaign to raise some vital funds for the charity. At the end of the crowdfunding campaign I had raised just over £2,000. I now present talks on "My Life Living with Asperger's" and recently organised and presented two of these talks at my squash club. I donated half of the money raised from these talks to Family Equip. My grandad also chose Family Equip as his charity when he was captain of his golf society. Between us we raised a few hundred pounds. The work that the charity does is vital and a lifeline to many individuals and their families. However, it is often small charities like Family Equip that do not get the help and support that the larger charities get. Yet, charities like this are vital to the individuals and families that they support.

Recently Family Equip put together a promotional video. The video was about the work that the charity carries out and the benefits to the individuals and families that it helps. My dad and I were interviewed for the video and I talked about what having Asperger's is like to live with and how the charity has helped me over the years. My dad talked about what it is like being a parent of someone who has Asperger's. This video was used to apply for some funding, and I hope our interviews helped show what amazing work the charity carries out.

"Help yourself by helping others."

John Templeton

CHAPTER 19
Sixth form

"77% of young people with special educational needs such as autism who take A-Levels or equivalent exams will go on to higher education, employment or training."

Ambitious About Autism, Stats and facts

As soon as I started sixth form, I felt a lot happier and a lot more relaxed. I had more flexibility, I only did subjects that I enjoyed and I had more free time. I was also allowed to wear my own clothes, so instead of suppressing my personality, as I had been made to do in my school uniform, I could now express my personality. These were the things that my dad had said I needed as soon as I first started the school at the age of eleven and he was proven to be right because I felt a lot happier.

I was in sixth form for two years and the two subjects that I took for A-Levels were ICT (information and communications technology) and DT (design and technology). They were not my best subjects but the subjects which I enjoyed the most.

In my first year there were four people in my ICT class and four people in my DT class. However, in my second year there were only three people in my ICT class and two people in my DT class. As you can tell, it was a very small sixth form!

Wednesday afternoons were used for enrichment where the students could sign up for a number of different activities. When I was in Years 10 and 11 my first enrichment activity was squash where we would go and play at Edgbaston Priory. My second enrichment activity was golf at Edgbaston Golf Club. My English teacher used to take us to play golf and we once both wore the same coloured pink trousers! In sixth form I started to volunteer at the Birmingham Botanical Gardens where I worked in the shop and plant sales. I used to go there every Wednesday afternoon for about a year. My ambition at the time was to be a garden designer and I even looked into the horticultural courses that they did there.

My ICT teacher said that I knew the subject better than any other pupil she had ever had and I knew our text book inside out. However, in my final exam, when I was expected to get an A, I got a D. It was not because I did not know the subject well enough but because I did not understand any of the questions. It was like I was doing an exam on a completely different subject. Exams are one thing that people with Asperger's can really struggle with. If the questions are not clear or if they are ambiguous, then we don't have a clue what to write, even if in reality we know the answer. Also, our ICT textbooks took seven weeks to arrive. The teacher put in two orders that the other members of staff never sent off, and it was only on the third order that the books were sent off for. In the meantime, the teacher had to photocopy pages from the one book that she did have.

During my second year of DT our main teacher decided to leave. Because the only other DT teacher in the school could not fill in her lessons, the school had to find an external DT teacher to come in one afternoon a week to teach me and my friend. He was a really good teacher, but because we only had him once a week, we had only that one afternoon to ask him questions and to get any help on the subjects that he was teaching us. Also, because the afternoon he came in was on a Wednesday, which I usually spent volunteering at the Botanical Gardens, it meant I had to give this up. I was a little annoyed at the time, but I knew that my A-Levels were more important.

We also had a few other problems with DT. The A3 printer in the DT block never seemed to work and we had to wait weeks for new cartridges to arrive. This meant that I had to draw my work on ordinary paper and cut and stick it on to the correct A3 paper that had my borders on. The printer also started blurring the page borders and images as well as producing black lines across the pages. We had a

3D printer in the DT block as well, but it either did not work or the teachers did not know how to use it. This meant that I had to handmake my presentation box instead of the printer doing it for me. To be honest, I was not confident with any of the printers in the school and would have been worried that any printer I used would not have printed my work properly. The DT building had no heating, mouse mats that were broken, mice that were sticky as the rubbers had come off, and two classrooms that shared the same lighting system. As you can see, for me there were a number of disadvantages from being at a small private school. The advantages that many parents think their children receive from a private education aren't always delivered on. These problems were not unique to the DT department as there were similar problems throughout the whole school. I think it is important for parents to thoroughly investigate the facilities provided before choosing subjects.

Unfortunately, my teaching assistant, who I had been with since Year 7, left during my final year at the school, which was also my last year in the sixth form. There was no replacement, so I had practically nobody that I felt that I could talk to. Another teacher at the school who many of my friends and I would go and talk to was the librarian. She had started off as a teaching assistant in some of my lessons when she had first arrived at the school and had ended up becoming the school's librarian. I felt comfortable talking to her and when she also left in my last year it really did leave me with nobody that I could talk to!

I also discovered that other students were not getting the extra support in lessons from teaching assistants that they were entitled to and needed. I raised this issue in a school council meeting, but as the Headteacher had just walked in, they did not want it to be discussed. At the time the Headteacher was showing two new teachers around the school. They were asked how many teaching assistants they had in their current schools and for how many students. The Headteacher said we should be grateful for the support we receive. However, I felt this missed the point because it mattered how many people in their schools had Statements and extra support requirements. My point is that the council were paying the school to provide the resource outlined in our Statements. In some cases, we were not receiving this level of support. As a student I had the ability to recognise the real issues that were being ignored by others. My advice to parents is that you must check that your child is receiving the support outlined in the Statement that the council is paying for. A child with Asperger's will probably not think to tell you!

The sixth form study rooms were very small and noisy, and I found that I just could not work in them. Instead, if I had any free periods I used to go to the library. When it came to the end of the school year when all of the exams took place, not only was the library out of use because exams were going on in there but so were the sixth form rooms. Sometimes the only free classroom in the whole school was the politics room, which was very small and only had one computer. When eight sixth formers were in there at the same time it became very cramped. Sometimes, even this room was being used and so the only free space to work was on the tables outside. This was a particular problem for the students with Asperger's.

I still attended the Den (lunch club) whilst I was in the sixth form, playing table tennis most lunchtimes. During my first year of sixth form they tried to close the Den which everyone involved was very upset about. They said that they wanted us to go outside and mix with other year groups, but we went outside every breaktime anyway. Also, the Den was the one place where your age did not matter and you often saw different year groups playing together. I was in the sixth form and I often played table tennis with some of the Year 7s. Some of the people who went there found it was the only part of the school day they enjoyed. Instead of just accepting that it had closed, we protested. Every breaktime six or eight of us would stand by the Den and refuse to leave. Then at lunchtime we would march around the school grounds with "Save the Den" posters chanting, "Save the Den!" During this period, I even wrote a letter to the top of the school about how much the Den meant to us all and why it should not be closed. I actually feel that this was one of the best pieces of writing I have ever written. Most people used to think that I was the reason for saving the Den, but in actual fact it was all started by my friend who was two years younger than me. I was just the one who carried this on! All schools should have somewhere like the Den for children to go during lunchtimes and breaktimes. For many children with Asperger's school is particularly stressful at these unstructured times of the day and it is important to have a safe place to go to spend time with friends.

When it was approaching my last few weeks at the school, it was time for me to start thinking about my next step and what I wanted to do once I left. I looked at some of the horticultural courses that they did at the Botanical Gardens, but after attending an open day there decided that it was TV presenting that I wanted to pursue. I had seen a Specialist Careers Advisor from the council a few times, as had some of my friends. She had spoken to me before I started GCSEs, during my time at sixth form and then towards the end of my time at sixth form. I had also put together a short document mapping out all the things about me, my ambitions, the work experience I had gained and my contingency plans to try and help me with my next choice.

During the summer of 2015, about two months after I had finished sixth form, I had three days of travel training with a man called Adam from our local council. My parents wanted me to learn how to use public transport to get to places such as the Mailbox in Birmingham, my squash, golf and table tennis clubs and my grandparent's house. On the first two days, I was taught how to get the train from my house to the Mailbox. We would have done this on the third day as well but I also wanted some help with getting buses. I found it harder getting buses than I did getting trains. So, on the third day, I was shown how to get the bus from my house to the college that I was going to as well as to my golf club. It was really helpful and I felt a lot more confident in getting trains on my own. I still felt a bit nervous getting buses, but I felt more confident than I had done to begin with. I think this "Travel Training" programme is a great initiative by the council. Recently, I was asked to help a younger boy, from Family Equip, with "travel training". I spent a couple of days helping him catch the train and I think it really helped him.

"The only way to do great work is to love what you do. If you haven't found it yet, keep looking. Don't settle. As with all matters of the heart, you'll know when you find it."

Steve Jobs

CHAPTER 20
Helping me to de-stress

"Stress is often described as one of the major barriers to a fulfilled life for autistic people. It affects people across the autism spectrum at all stages of their lives. Of course, stress affects everyone, but there is growing awareness that autistic people may be particularly susceptible to high levels of unhealthy stress."

National Autistic Society,
Reflections on stress and autism

Over the years I have found many ways to de-stress that help me to calm down, whether that be at home, at school or out in public. When I am having a meltdown, for example, I have a different strategy at home to when I was at school or when I am out in public. I still use most of these strategies today. Before I was diagnosed with Asperger's I would always carry a bag around with me containing all sorts of items. These ranged from a mini-screwdriver to hairbrushes, torches, pens, books etc. If ever I was stressed, I would just go straight into my bag and start rummaging around. My family often used to ask me for items that they needed and usually I would have them.

When I was first diagnosed with Asperger's the teacher at my primary school, who I used to see for five minutes every morning, helped me to make three cards that I used to look at when I was stressed. These cards had images of footballers on them as well as motivational sayings. Whenever I was in a lesson and I started to feel stressed I could look at these cards quietly without anybody noticing. Sometimes looking at these cards would prevent me from needing a "time out", which I was only allowed three times a week. Whatever it is that someone with Asperger's is interested in, having something to do with their favourite subject that they can look at can be very helpful. I am interested in football, so looking at footballers used to de-stress me, whereas one of my friends who likes trains would look at photos of trains to help him de-stress.

At primary school when I had a "time out" I would give the teacher one of the three counters that I had, and she would then know what was happening. I would go to a quiet place for five or ten minutes and start reading one of my football programmes. The football programmes always used to de-stress me and reminded me of the matches that I had been to. To this day, I still carry a football programme with me wherever I go in case I have some free time or I start to feel stressed. These "time outs" were a lifeline because if I ever got my football programmes out in lessons, I would have some of the girls in my class telling tales which used to make me even more stressed than I had been in the first place! The school should not have limited the number of "time outs" I was allowed to three as this caused additional stress. I would always be worrying about what I would do if I ran out of them.

When I moved to secondary school, I used to keep a small photo album in my blazer pocket containing images of my family. Then, just like with the football cards at primary school, I could get my photos out and start looking at them when I became stressed. We were not allowed phones in lessons, so this was the next best alternative. Looking at the photos of my family made me think about the good times I had had with them and took my mind away from school for those few moments.

At secondary school I also used to ring my dad if I became stressed at school, although only at breaktimes or lunchtime. When I was talking to him it felt like I was communicating with the outside world and he always used to calm me down. Also, he was the one person that I knew would always be available to talk. Some of the teachers knew that I would phone my dad if I was stressed, but others did not. These teachers would usually tell me off and make me put my phone away. For that reason, I had to watch out if any teachers were coming, and usually I made the phone calls to my dad from towards the bottom end of the school grounds. As it was such a small school, I feel that all of the teachers should have known about this. They could have been told in their daily briefing sessions that they had in the staff room.

As I explained earlier, one small incident coming home from school could often be enough to cause a release of all the tension that had been building up throughout the day and for me to have a meltdown. One thing that has always calmed me down is children's television. When I was younger my mum would always try and put CBeebies on the TV, but I would always try and stop her. However, when she did manage to get it on it was like a magic wand had been waved over me and, instantly, I was transfixed by the television. All the anger and stress would seem to go in an instant. This is also a good strategy when I am having a meltdown. Nowadays I can feel when I am having a meltdown and I can go and put a children's programme on myself.

Again as I explained earlier, chocolate too is also something that can help me to de-stress or recover from a meltdown. It seems to take the edge off any hunger I have, which helps.

I play a lot of sport, including squash and golf. I started playing squash when I was about seven and golf when I was about ten, and for many years I have been a member of Robin Hood Golf Club and Solihull Arden Squash Club. Sport is another way to relieve my stress as I feel completely relaxed when playing these sports. I know it is not always practical or possible to go and play sport when I'm stressed, but if I can then I will. When I am on a squash court there is nothing to distract me and all I am thinking about is hitting the ball with the racket. Also, hitting the ball and running around helps me to get some of the anger or stress out, plus it actually makes me play better. So, exercise is a great way to release your frustrations and stress.

Some of my friends find that punch bags are good to use when they are stressed because they can let all of their anger out on the bag instead of breaking or throwing items or verbally abusing their family. Having something to fidget with can also lessen our anxiety or tension. When I was at school I was always fiddling with my pens, taking them apart and putting them back together. I guess this was a subconscious way to stop myself from getting stressed. For others, they may like to fiddle with a stress ball, a fidget spinner or something else. One of the common things to help us relax and reduce our stress levels is listening to music. I would often listen to music in the taxi and in some of my GCSE English lessons if I was feeling stressed.

"You can succeed in whatever it is you want to do. Don't let your circumstances define you and never give up."

Alex Manners

CHAPTER 21
Football and specialist interests

"Most people with autism have particular favourite subjects. Special interests can simply be like hobbies or careers only more so: someone on the spectrum can dedicate an immense amount of time to their special interest, even dedicating every free moment to it."

Ambitious About Autism,
Obsessions and special interests

Many people with Asperger's have a specialist subject or interest that they are obsessed with, such as trains and spades to name just two. They may be common interests, such as football, but often they can be very specific and unusual. These subjects dominate our every thought and we tend to know our specialist interest in great depth. One of my Asperger friends is obsessed with bins, like wheelie bins and skips, and to a non-autistic person you may think that that is a little odd. But let me tell you, he is one of the cleverest people I know and is currently at university studying chemical engineering. I met him on the train recently and the first thing he said to me was, "Do you have any pictures of bins on your phone?" I have now found myself researching about bins on the internet and watching the binmen out of my window at home. Whatever someone might be interested in, however unusual or obscure, it may be beneficial for their everyday life and a way of coping with their struggles. And, at the end of the day, they could get a job off the back of their special interest. Indeed, some of the richest men in the world have arguably got Asperger's and have made their fortune from being totally focused on their passion. They say that Albert Einstein and Isaac Newton may have had Asperger's.

I am absolutely obsessed with football. I go to bed thinking about football and wake up thinking about football. It dominates my every thought. My bedroom walls are lined with pennants and posters from all the different teams and grounds I have visited. My wardrobe is full of all the football treasures that I have collected over the years, shirts, programmes, scarves, you name it. When I was younger, I used to collect Top Trump cards, Monsters in My Pocket, McDonalds toys and many sticker albums, so clearly, I have a trait of collecting things. I can name every ground name in the top five tiers of English football. That is 116 grounds that I know the names of. Every spare moment that I have will be spent researching these grounds and many others to keep up to date with their names, capacities, developments etc. I am also trying to visit all 92 English Football League grounds for a match and, as of February 2019, I have currently completed 89 of them. Over the years, my love of football has allowed me to overcome some of the difficulties that my Asperger's has thrown up and has given me another focus in life.

During my quest to "do the 92" my Uncle Tim has taken me up and down the country watching football matches, and I am forever grateful for the amount of time and effort he has given to allow me to achieve my dream. Without him I would be nowhere near completing the 92. My Uncle Tim took me to my first ever game in 2007. It was Birmingham City against Hereford United and from that game onwards I was hooked; I had caught the football bug. It was not until a few years later when I decided to add up all the grounds I had been to that I decided that I would like to try and do the 92. At the time, I think I had done about 30 of them. My Uncle Tim often jokes that I only attend the matches to see the mascots and the club shops. This is because whatever ground we go to I always know where the club shop is located and who the club's mascots are.

If you think of someone who is always on edge, then that is how I am with football. No matter where I am or how obscure the reference is, if there is something to do with football then I will notice it. I was with my uncle at his tennis club the other week, and as we were sitting in the bar, I noticed the one and only advertising board outside on one of the courts. I thought, "That is unusual. I am sure that that company, Benenden, sponsors the York City FC shirts." When I checked on Google, sure enough I was right. I don't know how I knew that, but that is how obsessed I am with football. I have even started an "Autism and Football" campaign to enhance the experience of autistic people at football matches. Recently, I was interviewed by ITV Central after my visits to the Arsenal and Watford FC sensory facilities.

At school I started to bring football in to every lesson and would always find a way of bringing some element of football in to each piece of work. I would even put football badges on pieces of work that had nothing to do with football. In one Year 7 ICT lesson I made a PowerPoint presentation about hardware and software. I inserted three football badges onto the front of this presentation. It was my way of trying to cope with school and all its stresses and worries that I talked about earlier. In one particular science lesson we had to create our own planets. As I had just been to watch Luton Town the previous weekend, I made a planet called Pluton. It was the planet Pluto with the Luton Town crest in the middle. One of the teachers even said that if I knew as much about the work as I did about football then I would get top marks.

I always found that I enjoyed the creative subjects such as DT more than the academic subjects like maths and English. With creative subjects there are more opportunities to bring in our favourite or specialist subject. One of our DT projects in Year 7 was to create our own theme park. I created one called "The Wacky Wembley Theme Park". Each ride was named after a different football club, and in the theme park leaflet that I made I included all of the different team badges. Then in Year 9 we had to make lamps. I designed and made my lamp in the shape of a football.

I always find that football is a great conversation starter. After introducing myself the next thing I would ask someone is, "Do you like football?" or "Do you support a football team?" As football is such a popular subject, even if they don't necessarily follow football, they will probably have some understanding of it. And then I can be straight into a conversation without really having to think too much about it. Although people with Asperger's can find it hard to have a conversation, if they are talking about their specialist interest then they will often be able to talk very well and have a proper conversation. It's like our specialist subject is acting as a barrier breaker.

I have now taken my obsession with football a step further and during the 2016/17 and 2017/18 seasons I filmed all of the Solihull Moors home games for BT Sport's *Vanarama National League Highlights Show*. I was responsible for not only filming the matches but interviewed the managers at every game. I also have my own YouTube channel where I film "Around the Grounds" and "Football Shirt Story" videos and a website detailing my quest to do the 92.

"Focus on what you want, what you enjoy, and do it with passion and enthusiasm."

Unknown

CHAPTER 22
Children's TV

"58% of parents reported that Thomas & Friends was the first children's character their child liked. Almost 39% of parents reported that their child's interest in Thomas & Friends lasted over two years longer than siblings' interest in the character."

Verywell Health,
Thomas the Tank Engine and autism connection

I f you know me well, then you will know that I am a fan of CBeebies and shows such as *Noddy*, *Thomas the Tank Engine* and *Tweenies*. You may think that I am a little too old for shows like that, but why should my age stop me from watching them? If I enjoy them, then isn't that all that matters? I mean, I am not harming anyone by watching these shows. Quite a number of people with Asperger's will have a particular children's show that they like or that they find relaxing and calming. For me, these shows make me feel happy and they put a smile on my face. They are also a great way of de-stressing. As soon as I see one on the TV, I instantly feel relaxed and all the anger or worries seem to just disappear. They are also a great help when I am having a meltdown. When I was younger my mum would always try and put a children's programme on the TV, but now I am older I can put one on myself when I am having a meltdown. I have a few children's DVDs such as *Winnie the Pooh*, *In the Night Garden*, *Horrid Henry* and the *Cloudbabies* that I can watch in these situations.

I was watching a TV documentary about autism and during the show they were interviewing a boy who was about nineteen. He was interested in heavy metal and horror movies and was showing the camera his collection of horror DVDs. However, within his collection of horror movies was one children's DVD. I can't remember what the show was, but when the interviewer asked him why he had this particular DVD he said that it helped him to calm down when he was angry or stressed. Once in a French lesson at school we were asked to go on YouTube and watch some French videos. My friend and I spent the lesson watching *Noddy* videos in French. Not only did we really enjoy the lesson but it was also very funny and very relaxing.

Some of you may remember a show that used to be on CBeebies called *Tweenies*. This show has always been a personal favourite of mine. For a start, the whole show is just a world of colour and is really eye-catching. I mean, how can you not just feel happy when watching it? The characters are really simple to understand; they don't use any ambiguous sayings or phrases, you can always tell how they are feeling and they do not have complex storylines. In essence these kinds of programmes are easy for us to grasp and they don't leave us feeling confused.

When I was younger, I built up a big collection of Tweenies toys and merchandise, which I still have a lot of today. If I ever go swimming, then I will often take my Tweenies towel with me. When I was about ten my aunt gave me some fabric pens, which I used to draw some of my favourite CBeebies characters onto one of my plain white polo shirts. I had wanted to buy a shirt with some of my CBeebies favourites on, like the Tweenies or the Teletubbies. However, the only shirts like this that were on sale were for under fours and not for ten-year-olds. When I was older my mum took me to Drayton Manor Theme Park. Whilst we were there, we went into the Thomas Land shop as I wanted to see if they sold any adult-sized Thomas the Tank Engine shirts. They had no Thomas the Tank Engine shirts for adults on sale, but they did have three behind the counter that they had made for a trial. They were not for sale, but my mum persuaded the man to let us buy one.

When I was in the sixth form, I used to play a lot of table tennis. I had my own table tennis bag with my bats and balls in. My bag happened to be a Teletubbies bag that I had purchased from the Ragdoll shop in Stratford-Upon-Avon. I did not choose this bag deliberately because it had children's characters on but because it was a perfect fit for my table tennis equipment. Sometimes I used to take this bag into school if I had arranged to play with one of my friends during a free period. I'm sure some of the other pupils and even some of the teachers thought that a sixth former bringing in a Teletubbies bag was a little odd, but I did not mind what other people thought. Nobody ever said anything anyway.

In 2016, I attended a "CBBC Awesome Authors" event in Birmingham with my mum. I dressed up in my multi-coloured spotty trousers and shirt and even took a rainbow umbrella with me. The clothes were representing my character "Rainbow Man" who is the main character in the new children's show I had been writing. The event was absolutely fantastic and I got to meet some of the CBBC presenters who have been my idols for as long as I can remember. I met Sam Nixon and Mark Rhodes, Barney Harwood and Radzi Chinyanganya. I also went on stage with the *Match of the Day Kickabout* presenter Ben Shires to talk about my new show. It was a real confidence booster to meet Ben as he told me I had a great presence in front of the camera, and it gave me the push I needed.

The children's show that I've created is called "Rainbow Man". Rainbow Man is a fun and colourful children's television show that is aimed at under-fives to educate and encourage them to learn. Rainbow Man is supported by a fun and quirky narrator as well as memorable friends such as "Grumpy Doug" and "Giddy Gordon". These characters are based on my two grandads. Some of the values that are portrayed include empathy, self-esteem and creativity. During each show, Rainbow Man visits a different location and educates children on the world around them. Overall the show is aimed at being amusing, educational and visually exciting. I have created numerous documents on the show including presentations, scripts, style guides and videos.

I sent my "Rainbow Man" scripts and documents to the CBeebies commissioning team, who reviewed it in one of their commissioning meetings. Unfortunately, they did not choose to go ahead with the production of my show as they said that it was too similar to other shows that they already aired. I was disappointed, but just to have my show considered by CBeebies was a huge achievement in itself. I now read my "Rainbow Man" stories on my children's radio show that airs every Sunday morning from 8-10am on Solihull Radio (www.solihullradio.com). I have even introduced a new character called "Awesome Alex" who has Asperger's and is based upon myself. My radio show also includes children's music, stories, events for children and excerpts of old kids' TV shows.

My ambition is to be a television presenter for children and to create innovative children's shows. As I mentioned above, I even have my own children's radio show! I feel that my love of CBeebies and children's programmes allows me to better understand and empathise with the children watching them, and what better way to work in a job you love and know a lot about. I bet none of the current CBeebies presenters like watching the shows as much as I do!

"If you don't ask, you don't get."

Mahatma Gandhi

CHAPTER 23
College

"Fewer than one in four school leavers with autism stay in further or higher education."

Ambitious About Autism, Stats and facts

When I left sixth form my ambition had changed from wanting to be a garden designer to a TV presenter. My dad had paid for me to go on a TV presenter training course at the Custard Factory in Birmingham in 2015. From that one course, I realised that a job in TV was what I really wanted to do. It would be a way for me to express my personality and to wear my colourful clothes. Being a TV presenter would also give me a chance to do something that I would be remembered for. A normal nine-to-five job did not appeal to me. I had also started a YouTube channel, filming football videos on the matches and grounds I visited and on my collection of football shirts. These are some of the reasons why I decided to study creative media at college.

I was a little worried about going to college as it was a big change from the small sixth form I had previously been at. The college that I went to was very close to where I lived but was really big. I was especially worried about what people would think about the way in which I dressed i.e. my colourful clothes. Also, I was worried about making friends, as I thought the kind of people who would be in my class would be the kind of people who I would not get along with. I was going to be doing a completely different subject to the two I had done for A-Levels at sixth form. I did not go to college for the end qualification, as I knew that it was my personality and determination that would lead me to become a TV presenter and not a creative media qualification which anyone could get. Instead, I went to try and learn as much as I could about the media industry and especially things such as filming and editing.

It transpired that I need not have worried about going to college. For a start, everyone in my media class was really friendly and nobody had any issues with the clothes that I wore. I really enjoyed my first year in college and learnt quite a bit. However, my second year at the college was not quite so good and I ended up leaving a few months early. The main problem was that I was becoming unmotivated because I felt that I was not learning that much. Out of the 25 or so people in my class there was only one other person who was as motivated to achieve his ambitions as I was. The rest of the class seemed as though they were just there to fill up their time. For example, when the teacher asked us if we had got any work experience, I had got more than was required. Plus, as I had already started my own video production business, I had actually got paid for some of this work. The majority of people had not got any work experience. From what I gathered, they not only could not be bothered to get any but seemed not to want any.

Due to a combination of their attitudes and the fact that we were not learning much in class (or learning things that I did not see as relevant, such as film studies), I became really disillusioned. When I used to go into college, I would sit there thinking about all of the things I could be doing at home to advance my career. However, when I eventually did get home, I would not do any of these things because the day at college had dragged my motivation levels down. One of the pieces of work we had to do was to create a promotional video for a company. I had already finished my video. However, nobody else in my class had even started filming and some had not even thought of what they would be filming. When the teacher went around the class asking everyone about our projects, he left me out because he thought I was working in another group. That was the final straw and I left about a week or two after that.

The same teacher also complained to me about the filming I was doing outside of the college. The other class in our year had finished for the year, but this teacher made us come in for two extra lessons. In one of those lessons he was not even there for most of it. I told him that I needed to leave early because I had a filming job to do which I was being paid for. You would think he would have been pleased about this, but instead he told me that I should tell them that I can't film certain things when they clash with my lessons. The filming was more important to me anyway; plus it was not like I could film these videos when it suited me. If I was filming say a squash game, then if I did not film it at the time it was scheduled for, then I would not have filmed it at all.

Whilst we did learn a little bit about editing, we only had one lesson on how to use a camera. I did not even find this lesson useful because I had already been using these types of cameras to film the games with at Solihull Moors. Part of our course was to learn about film and cinematography. We had to watch a number of films for our course, and they all included torture, drugs, gangs or horror, my worst kind of movies. I hated watching them and to me those lessons were a complete waste of time. They actually made me feel uncomfortable, especially as I have a phobia of blood and needles. One particular piece of work we had to carry out involved us finding a news story to use. I was the only person in my class who did not choose a news story that involved a killing or some form of horrific crime. I chose a news story about the sacking of the then England manager Sam Allardyce.

I left the college about three months before my course was supposed to finish. I had wanted to leave about two months before this, but my dad had convinced me to stay. It had got to the point where I had just had enough and was very unhappy there, hence why I left. I still wanted to try and get the qualification if I could and went in to speak to one of the teachers about the work that I still needed to do, which I would then do from home. It took me about a day to complete the work that the rest of the class took three months to do and I still got the qualification. To be honest, I learnt more by myself in the six months after I left the college than I had done in the nearly two years I had spent at the college. My dad told me after I had left, and when I was progressing with my own business, that he was impressed with me for making the intelligent decision to leave college.

"Life is an adventure, so enjoy it."

Alex Manners

CHAPTER 24
Back to front

"There is continued debate about whether the autism spectrum should be seen as a form of difference or of disability. Most people we spoke to talked about feeling different. For some, this was a positive feeling while others described feeling isolated and wanting to fit in."

Healthtalk, Autism, feeling different
and wanting to fit in

The things that most people find hard, I find easy. The things that most people find easy, I find hard. I feel like I am different from most people and, as I would call it, "back to front". Because I have Asperger's, I think differently to most people. I can think of different ways of solving problems and I feel that this is a gift that has come from having Asperger's. I feel like I am from a different planet, "Planet Asperger's". Indeed, my dad often says this when he sees me with all my Asperger's friends. He says individually most of the group struggle to communicate or socialise but when we are with each other we chat away and laugh just like everyone else.

I present and produce my own children's radio show on Solihull Radio, my local radio station. You may find producing a whole radio show on your own very difficult. The sheer amount of equipment that you need to use and buttons that you need to press would baffle most people. But not me! I find producing my show very easy. Even before my first show, when it was the first time that I was going to be alone in the studio, I was not worried. My mum could not understand how I knew how to use all of the equipment, and my uncle said that he did not understand how I could present my own show as well as producing it. On the other hand, I can sometimes find having a conversation, and in particular "small talk", tricky. That is something that most people would find easy.

I often get the train in the morning and when I am at the station, I notice the amount of people travelling to work. To me they all look the same. All the men are either dressed in black suits, dark blue suits or grey suits. I never see a red suit or a yellow suit. Most of the people I see would never wear a red or a yellow suit. However, I would never wear a black, dark blue or a grey suit. Also, when I went to college the majority of the students were either in tracksuits or jeans, nearly always black or blue. I wonder why it is that everyone feels the need to dress in the same clothes and the same colours as everyone else. I am the opposite and probably look as different to everyone else as physically possible in my floral shirts and multi-coloured outfits!

As you know by now, as well as presenting my own radio show, I am a lover of football and travel up and down the country with my Uncle Tim watching matches every week. Uncle Tim supports Birmingham City. They are the only team he supports and the only team he is really ever bothered about. I guess most supporters are like this; some may have a second team that they look out for but no more than that. I support four teams, Birmingham City, Swansea City, Burton Albion and Solihull Moors. However, whatever match I am watching I will always support the team whose end I'm in. Not only do I usually know all of the club's songs, but my room is filled with pennants and posters of every team imaginable. The only football shirt that my uncle would wear is one from Birmingham City, but I collect football shirts and I honestly don't think that there is a club whose shirts I would refuse to wear.

Taking my driving test was a nightmare. I took and failed five tests in a manual car. It was not that I was a bad driver, but I always did one thing wrong that resulted in a fail. The rest of the tests were almost faultless. I found that having gears was giving me extra things to think about, and my mum thought that was the reason I was always making that one big mistake. We decided that for my sixth test I would take the test in my mum's automatic, and in her car, I passed on my first attempt. Because I didn't have any gears to worry about, I had more time to concentrate on the roads. I would definitely recommend anyone who has Asperger's to take their driving test in an automatic car. Multi-tasking is an issue for many people with Asperger's. Driving often involves multi-tasking as you often have to do several things at once, like steering and changing gear.

Another reason that I feel "back to front" is because, whilst I am always ready on time, I am always in a mad rush before I leave. I always like to know exactly what time I am leaving or need to leave by and even when I have loads of time to get ready in, I still end up rushing. Sometimes when I am working at home for the day and I am going out in the evening you would think that I had plenty of time to get ready. You would be wrong, and still five minutes before I leave, I am in a mad rush trying to get ready. I nearly always have to run to catch the train.

Recently, I was filmed by Channel 4 for something they were doing online called "Am I normal?" I was filmed for this at the Autism Show in London before I presented one of my talks. One of the points I made was about the colourful clothes I wear and how, when waiting for a train to go into Birmingham, I stand out from all the people going to work. Some might smile but some look at me like

I am a fool and it made me think: how can a colour define you as normal or not normal?

"Sometimes it is the people who no one imagines anything of who do the things that no one can imagine."

Alan Turing

CHAPTER 25

Why I look upon my Asperger's as something positive

"In May 2013, the company SAP announced its objective to have one percent of its global workforce represented by employees on the autism spectrum by 2020 (about 650 jobs)."

Fortune, 4th June 2018

I can't deny that my Asperger's has caused me a lot of stress over the past 22 years, but from the moment I was diagnosed with Asperger's syndrome at the age of ten I have viewed it as something positive. When I was first told that I had Asperger's it was by the SENCO at primary school, and my parents were given no warning that I would be told! Clearly, I knew nothing about it but my dad, immediately as we left the meeting, told me that it was a good thing and that a lot of our family had autistic traits. As I've mentioned before, he told me that it gave us special powers e.g. thinking differently. It is something that I will have for life, and so for this reason I prefer to focus on the many positive traits that have come from my Asperger's. I believe that my Asperger's makes me the person that I am today and will be responsible for my achieving my ambitions due to my unique strengths.

The reason I believe I will achieve my ambition to be a TV presenter is because I have a persistent and "never give up" attitude. My dad once told me that he believed I would achieve my ambition provided that I never give up. I replied, "Why would I give up when I know I am going to make it?" He laughed and said, "That's exactly why you're going to make it!" I have an internal motivation where I will not be swayed by what other people say, by social situations or by pressure. I hold firm to the things that I believe in and to my ambitions. Persistence comes naturally to me and is just one trait of my Asperger's. I am very single-minded and if I don't like something then I won't do it. While a lot of people end up in jobs that they don't enjoy, I would rather do nothing than spend day after day in a job that did not make me happy. I am determined to pursue my passion and to succeed and will persist until I do.

Whilst I don't feel that a nine-to-five would suit me, people with Asperger's can bring many benefits to companies. We are very thorough in the tasks we are given and will stay focused until they are completed, not letting anything distract us. This can allow us to accomplish large and challenging tasks. We also have great attention to detail and can remember and process a lot of information in minute detail and pick up on things that others may not notice. (This is why a lot of people with Asperger's are employed in the IT industry testing code.) My attention to detail means that in my bedroom everything has been carefully sorted and ordered, even down to individual boxes and pencil cases. I am a very logical thinker, and this can often lead me to carry out tasks or solve problems in very unusual yet logical ways. We also have very good memories, meaning that we can memorise large amounts of information for long periods of time. People with Asperger's can also be very conscientious, loyal, honest and logical.

I read an article recently about six big companies in America that have been looking at trying to employ people with Asperger's. The companies were Ford Motor, DXC Technology, EY, Microsoft, JPMorgan Chase and SAP. It quoted James Mahoney, Executive Director and Head of Autism at Work at Chase as saying, "Our autistic employees achieve, on average, 48% to 140% more work than their typical colleagues, depending on the roles." (*Fortune*, "Where autistic workers thrive", 4th June 2018)

It's clear that there needs to be a real focus by government on this issue of helping people with autism and Asperger's find proper long-term employment. There is no doubt that these people have a lot to offer, but they will need to be looked after in a work environment. The investment in looking after them will be far outweighed by the return that they will give a business in terms of their super skills, conscientious approach and loyalty.

If I enjoy a certain topic, then I want to know everything about it. I've talked about my obsession with football. My Asperger's leads me to exploring my hobbies in more depth than neurotypical individuals, and this is the reason why I have created quirky videos, such as "Around the Grounds" and "Football Shirt Stories", on my YouTube channel.

When I am being interviewed on the TV or the radio I never feel nervous. Most people would find being interviewed very difficult and my grandma said that she would not be able to eat for a week if she knew she was going on the radio. I, on the other hand, could stand up and talk in front of 100 or more people without any worries. To me, speaking in front of 100 people is no different than speaking in front of my parents. Also, being on live radio often means that I have to think fast when answering the questions, which, I have to say, I feel that I am pretty good at. Speaking to people who are in higher roles or who are famous never fazes me as I treat everybody the same. Similarly, when I am presenting a talk, I never feel nervous as I feel like I am talking to one person. Most of these people will have also been in my situation once upon a time before they became famous, so why should I feel nervous talking to them?

Another trait that I feel comes from my Asperger's is the empathy I feel for children. In some ways I think more like a child than I do an adult and I think this explains why I have a love for children's TV. Most twenty-two year olds wouldn't choose to watch CBeebies, but, as I've said, I really enjoy it. Shows such as the *Tweenies* or *In the Night Garden* are a form of escapism for me. I like the easy-to-understand vocabulary, which unlike adult language isn't full of hidden meanings e.g. idioms, sarcasm etc.

Having Asperger's has made me who I am today. A lot of my radio and TV interviews and articles that I have written have all been about my Asperger's, particularly what it is like living with it. Without Asperger's I would not have had nearly as much exposure to the TV world or gained nearly as many contacts. So, having Asperger's has helped me to grow my media network and may just be the catalyst that enables me to break into television.

"I will have Asperger's for life, so I prefer to focus on its positives and not its negatives."

Alex Manners

CHAPTER 26
My ambition to be a TV presenter

"I've spent 30 years on the telly trying my best to act normal ..."

Chris Packham quoted in *The Telegraph*, 9th October 2017 (just one of the many people with autism who have successful careers in TV, such as Anne Hegerty or Guy Martin)

My first big break into the TV and media world came when I applied for the *Top Gear* co-presenter's job in the summer of 2015. Even though I didn't get chosen, it led on to lots of other things. The day after I finished sixth form, I was down in Wimbledon with my Uncle Tim watching the tennis and our friend sent a message to my dad saying that he had seen me in the *Times* newspaper. When I looked in the paper, I was in an article all about the *Top Gear* auditions. My photo was the largest, in the centre of the article. I then went on to have articles written about my *Top Gear* audition in the *Birmingham Mail* and *Solihull News* as well as appearing for 40 minutes on BBC WM's *Sunny and Shay* show. I was even recognised by people when I went into my local town centre.

Since my audition for *Top Gear*, I managed to do some work experience at Big Centre TV (now Made in Birmingham) in Walsall, watching and helping to produce episodes of *Bostin Bear*, a programme for children. I was also a runner on a show called *Cuppa TV*. I was responsible for collecting the guests from reception and ensuring that they filled out the correct forms. I went in once a week for about six weeks and really enjoyed my time there. I had got in touch with Big Centre TV through a former TV presenter who was a member at my golf club. He told me the person to get in touch with at the station, and that is how I obtained the work experience. A lot of the time, I feel that it's not about what you know but who you know. I have also shadowed Paul Franks, the sports presenter on BBC WM, and did a week of work experience at the BT Sport studios in London. At BT Sport I helped to produce an episode of *Rugby Tonight*, was a runner for a Bundesliga football match and helped to produce *The Clare Balding Show*. I even got to go on stage with Clare and was a stand in during the rehearsals.

Somebody once told me that if I could use my Asperger's as a way to get an opportunity then I should do so. I should not flaunt it to people all the time, but it was mine to use at the right moment! From this piece of advice, I started to wonder whether I could start talking about my Asperger's. So, during Autism Awareness Week in 2016 (26th March - 2nd April), after sending numerous emails to TV and radio stations, I had a phone call to see if I would like to talk about my Asperger's on BBC Coventry and Warwickshire. When I got the phone call, I was playing golf with my grandparents in Wales as we were on holiday. My grandparents agreed to come home a day early, so that afternoon we drove back home. The next day my parents took me into the BBC Coventry and Warwickshire radio studios, and I was interviewed about my Asperger's live on air for about 30 minutes. A few days later I was interviewed live on *Big News* at Big Centre TV, again about my Asperger's. It was the first time I had been live on the TV and I loved every second of it.

I will never give up trying to achieve my dream, and if it takes me till I'm 60 to achieve it, then so be it. If I'm not working towards achieving my dreams and ambitions, then I can become quite miserable. That is why I always try and keep myself busy. Every day I am emailing people and working on different projects. No matter how big or small or famous somebody is the worst that anybody can say to you is "No". That is why I contact so many current TV personalities and presenters. I have had emails from Michael Portillo and Fiona Bruce, and I have connected with CBeebies presenters and *Strictly Come Dancing* professionals on LinkedIn. One of my ambitions is to be on *Strictly Come Dancing* one day. Every time that I meet somebody new, I will see if they are on LinkedIn and will try and connect with them if they are. Connecting with people on LinkedIn is one way for me to build up my network.

I am not particularly driven by money, but I do see it as a way to gauge how well I am doing with my career. The more money that I earn will mean the more talks I am presenting, the more awareness I am raising for Asperger's and the more people will get to know me and who I am. To be honest, I think I would rather be famous than rich. As far as earning a living is concerned, I don't want to go to work. Instead, I prefer to go on an adventure!

I have applied for many opportunities in the past, such as auditioning to become the new Cadbury Milk Tray Man. I've applied for a BBC Production Apprenticeship and to be a BBC Kick Off sports reporter. When I went in for the sports reporter interview, they actually said that I had too much experience for the role. Some people say that I work too hard, but as I see it, the more I work the closer I am to achieving my dream. I try to stop working at 9pm every evening. I see this as my cut off point and my time to relax. If it gets to, say, 7 or 8pm and I do an extra hour of work, then I believe I am one hour closer to achieving my dreams. However, if I read a book or play a board game for that hour instead, then I feel like I have not achieved anything.

In June 2016, I found out that the *Antiques Roadshow* was coming to Baddesley Clinton, a local National Trust property. My grandparents and I decided that we would go and take some of our items with us to see if they were worth anything with a view to me getting on TV. We took one of my grandma's paintings, one of my grandad's old woodworking tools, my dad's stamp collection and an old fashion book that my grandma had found at the top of her wardrobe. She had not even looked at it for about twenty years. One of the first items that we went to have valued was the fashion book, which dated from around 1825. We sat down with the expert, and after talking to him he told us that he would like to see if there was a film crew around who would interview us for the programme. He liked my flowery shirt and thought that it tied in very nicely with the book. When he came back, he told us that a film crew would be ready to film us in about an hour.

In the meantime, not only did my grandma have to tell me everything she knew about the book but I made it my mission to try and get a photo with Fiona Bruce, the *Antiques Roadshow* presenter. I saw her on the central bandstand with lots of people around her. My grandad thought I would not get a photo with her, but I was determined that I would. She was in a bit of a rush but was happy to have a photo with me and even called me a "cool dude". Soon afterwards, I was interviewed for the show on my own, as my grandma did not want to be on the TV and later that year I appeared on the *Antiques Roadshow* on the TV.

Another opportunity that I managed to take advantage of happened when I was in a lesson at college. My mum was listening to BBC WM, the *Sunny and Shay* show, on the way home from work when she heard that they had a ticket for a play that night. They wanted somebody to go to it and then talk about the play on their programme the next day. My mum phoned me up to tell me about it and I phoned the BBC straightaway, who told me that I had been chosen for the ticket. That evening my mum and I went to the Alexandra Theatre in Birmingham to watch *American Idiot* and the next day I was interviewed live on BBC WM talking about the play. I was interviewed alongside two members of the cast, Amelia Lilly and Newton Faulkner. One of the two presenters, Shay, called me their "resident reviewer".

"If you choose a job you love, you will never have to work a day in your life."

Unknown

CHAPTER 27
Starting my own business

"Only 16% of autistic adults in the UK are in full-time paid employment, and only 32% are in some kind of paid work."

The National Autistic Society, Autism facts and history

My dad had bought me a video camera and I had started to film football videos for my new YouTube channel. The videos that I produced were "Around the Grounds" and "Football Shirt Stories". This was my first experience of filming, editing and producing my own videos. I had told my squash coach at Solihull Arden Club about my videos and it transpired that he asked me if I could film a video for him. After filming two videos for my coach, the club approached me to ask if I would film some videos for them. I now film all of the videos that the club put out on social media. I film squash, racketball, tennis, fitness classes, social events, tournaments etc. As a normal nine-to-five job was not for me, I decided to start my own business creating promotional videos for other sports clubs and companies. Initially I just focused on sports clubs, and some days I would spend hours phoning and emailing all of the local sports clubs in and around Solihull and Birmingham.

For me, a normal nine-to-five job would be awful and would probably leave me feeling depressed and completely unmotivated. Unless I was doing a job that I really enjoyed or that could lead me to where I wanted to be, I would feel as though I had failed. I just don't see the point in doing a job you don't enjoy, and I live by the maxim "Pursue your passion." I want to do a job that I enjoy and that I will be remembered for. I am not fazed by hard work and in my opinion the harder a job is to get, the more rewarding it will be once you have got it. One trait of my Asperger's is that I can't wear dark-coloured clothes. If I am wearing black or grey, for example, then I can become depressed and feel like I am hiding my personality. However, if I am wearing colourful clothes, then I feel as though I can conquer anything. As so many jobs require you to wear a certain uniform then this aspect would be a real struggle for me.

Over the last two years since I started my business I have not only filmed videos for sports clubs but also for companies. I have filmed videos for tennis, golf and football clubs, cricket companies, retail shops and pre-school groups. I have even filmed some horse racing videos for a local horse racing trainer. The videos that I have filmed have varied from time-lapse videos to function and event videos. I really enjoy filming, and it is also a good way to become better known within the media industry. Also, if I know as much as possible about what goes on behind the camera, then I will be better in front of the camera.

Whilst I was at college, one of the teachers approached me to see if I would like to be involved with filming the Solihull Moors home games for BT Sport after the club's promotion to the top tier of non-league football. She knew how passionate I was about football and that I had a lot of experience with filming and thought I would be one of the best suited to take up the opportunity. I dived at the chance and along with three other students we agreed to do it. Before we started filming the games, we all went down for two days in London. All the other participants who would be filming the other clubs home games were there as well. BT Sport chooses local college and university students to film their local clubs' games as a work experience opportunity. The footage that we film is then shown on a *Match of the Day*-type programme called the *Vanarama National League Highlights Show* that airs on a Sunday evening on BT Sport 1. On the first day in London we all got to film a pre-season friendly between Dagenham and Redbridge and Leyton Orient. On the second day we were taken to the BT

Sport studios to learn more about what we would be doing.

I had been watching Solihull Moors for a number of seasons, so to now be working with them was fantastic. For the 2016/17 and 2017/18 seasons, I filmed all of the Solihull Moors Saturday home games as well as interviewing the home and away managers after every game. After filming the match and the interviews I would then go onto the BT Sport laptop, which they had provided us with, to edit the highlights. I would clip out all of the goals and best moments from the game and edit them into one clip, which I would then send over to BT Sport along with the interviews. Since my work for BT Sport I have been asked to create several videos for Solihull Moors. I have created end of season highlights videos for the last two seasons as well as a corporate video for them.

So, whilst my main ambition is to be a TV presenter, running my own video production business is great for a number of different reasons. For a start, I really enjoy creating videos. It is also a good way to network with and meet people. You never know how useful those contacts may be in the future. It's giving me some great experience that will be valuable to me in the future. It is also a great way to earn some money whilst I pursue my ambition. You never know this could be the avenue that is responsible for my ambition being achieved. I never let a "No" faze me and will just keep searching until

I get a "Yes". I know it's extremely hard to set up your own company, but I am determined to have a life doing things I enjoy and "pursuing my passions".

"It is hard to fail, but it is worse never to have tried to succeed."

Theodore Roosevelt

CHAPTER 28
Asperger's champion

"A Sensory Room is a specially designed room which combines a range of stimuli to help individuals develop and engage their senses. These can include lights, colours, sounds, sensory soft play objects, aromas all within a safe environment that allows the person using it to explore and interact without risk."

Experia, The benefits of a sensory room

As I've explained, unlike many people who have Asperger's, I find having conversations easy and I don't get nervous when speaking in front of lots and lots of people. This is one of the reasons why I want to share my experiences of living and growing up with Asperger's with others. Many people who do speak about autism or Asperger's are either professionals or people who have family members with it and so do not have it themselves. Having Asperger's means that I can tell people exactly what having Asperger's is like and relay real life stories that I have experienced and been through. No one knows more than me about what it feels like to have Asperger's, so I am an expert in my field.

I have written a number of articles on my Asperger's for organisations such as Autism Together or Autism West Midlands, and for *Autism Parenting Magazine* and *SEN Magazine*. And as I've mentioned, I have also been interviewed about my Asperger's a number of times on the TV and radio (on BBC WM, BBC Coventry and Warwickshire, Big Centre TV and ITV Central).

Having attended football matches weekly since 2007, I know exactly what it is like for autistic fans at football matches and the areas that we can struggle with when going to games. I got in contact with an autistic charity in the South of England to see if I could help with their campaign to make football more autism friendly. Unfortunately, they already had a few people with autism helping them, so there were no opportunities for me to be involved. I consequently decided to set up my own campaign to nationally enhance the experience of autistic people at football matches.

The noises, smells and crowds inside and outside the football grounds, as well as the close proximity of people and seats, can often be too much to cope with. No two match days are the same, and having so many different variations on everyday normalities can be difficult as people with autism do not know what to expect. Many parents of autistic children have had to leave games early in order to relieve their child of the stress and anxiety that the match day experience was causing them. Most, if not all, football clubs have designated areas and seats for disabled fans and people who have "physical disabilities". However, the majority of clubs don't have any areas for people who have "hidden disabilities", such as autism, and many people's attitude to it is that if they can't see a problem then there must not be one! However, there are a number of ways that clubs can help autistic people, and many are starting to take notice and put things in place.

Conducting research, I contacted a number of football clubs, including Rangers and Middlesbrough, to ask them about what they were doing to help their autistic fans. I even went down to Arsenal FC in London and I was given a tour around their sensory room (a special room for autistic people). I was also shown round the sensory room at Watford. Arsenal then invited me down to watch a match from their sensory facilities, and I have to say that the person in charge of those facilities is the most knowledgeable person I have ever met when it comes to understanding autism. After speaking to the many different clubs that I contacted I put a research document together and I sent it to *SEN Magazine,* who published it as an article.

I then started to work on some projects with my local football club, Solihull Moors. Although they are only a small club, they have a wonderful attitude towards people with disabilities, not only when it comes to watching football but also playing football. They have an Ability Counts section which has over 75 players. One project involved me carrying out a survey with some of the club's autistic players from their Ability Counts section. Also, I created an "Autism Sensory Story" for the club. This is a series of images accompanied by words showing an autistic person images of the ground so they know what the match day experience at the club will be like prior to a game. Due to my campaign and the work I have been doing at the club, I was interviewed about my campaign by ITV Central at the Solihull Moors ground. As well as the campaign, I have put together an idea for a TV documentary and I currently have two TV production companies looking to produce a documentary on autism and football in relation to the research that I have carried out.

I now carry out talks on "My Life Living with Asperger's" and have presented my talk to places such as Warwick University, Solihull Council and the Autism Shows in both London and Birmingham. I have even put together separate talks on my time at school which I present to teachers and people who work in schools, a "positivity talk" which I present to students, and a talk on how football clubs can help their autistic fans. My talks usually last for about 40 minutes with time for Q & A afterwards, but this can always be adapted.

To coincide with my talk at the Autism Show in London, I added the new character to my "Rainbow

Man" stories called "Awesome Alex". This character has Asperger's syndrome and is based upon myself and my experiences of living with Asperger's. Awesome Alex shows how people with Asperger's function in different environments and will hopefully help raise awareness and understanding. I read a new "Rainbow Man" story every Sunday morning on my children's radio show that I present on Solihull Radio from 8-10am.

"I want to be able to look back and say, 'I did, not I could have!'"

Unknown

CHAPTER 29
My life now

"Seventy per cent of autistic adults say that they are not getting the help they need from social services. Seventy per cent of autistic adults also said that with more support they would feel less isolated."

The National Autistic Society, Autism facts and history

I am determined to "pursue my passion" and have a life doing things that I enjoy. Whether that be through video production, Asperger's talks, TV or radio, I will never give up! I know that most people with Asperger's would not be able to work on their own and set up their own business as it's extremely difficult and would not suit them. However, people with Asperger's must pursue their own passions, e.g. coding, gardening, research etc. in order to lead a fulfilled life. To enable this to happen, businesses need to recognise that they can be very valuable in the workplace, and I hope that with more awareness companies will start to see that these people can become their most valued employees.

From the age of two or three, I was always saying, "That's not right!" Once I was buying a football in a sports shop with my dad and they had put the wrong price on it. My dad thought that I was going to kick off because I was saying, "That's not right! This is the price, and I want to speak to Tony Blair." The staff were completely bemused and did not have a clue what was going on. My dad almost thought that they might call security. The world around me seemed confusing and nothing seemed to make sense. My way of expressing that to my parents was by saying, "That's not right!" Now, with the benefit of hindsight, my parents believe this was the first recognisable sign of my Asperger's. With more awareness, they think I would have been diagnosed at an earlier age and consequently would have benefited from the earlier help I would have received.

There is a lot of help and support for children with autism. I know I received a lot of help when I was diagnosed as a child and when I went to school (albeit not as good as it could have been). However, when we become adults that help and support suddenly stops. As we become adults our autism does not vanish as it is a lifelong condition. We just go from being autistic children to autistic adults, so why does the support stop?

Whilst I was in sixth form, three of my friends and I were talking to a teacher about our autism. We were specifically talking about some of the things we found stressful and the ways we cope with our stresses. Two of my friends present had autism, but one of my friends did not have autism. My friend who did not have autism said that he could not relate to the things we were talking about so instead went and played on the whiteboard. He was not being rude or trying to be awkward; he just could not understand what we were talking about. This hit home to me how different we were.

I really enjoy all of the work that I do, whether it be creating videos, writing articles or conducting talks on my Asperger's or presenting my own children's radio show on Solihull Radio. To be honest, my work does not actually feel like work because I enjoy everything I do. My life feels like one big adventure. I am determined to spend my life "pursuing my passions" and I endeavour to earn a living from doing so. I have the ability to inspire and motivate people and there is nothing more satisfying, so I feel very lucky to be able to do this.

Having Asperger's has had its challenges, but I believe it makes me who I am today and it will be the catalyst that allows me to achieve my dreams and ambitions. Whatever your circumstances are, never let them define you. If you are prepared to put the hard work in, then you can achieve anything.

"All our dreams can come true – if we have the courage to pursue them."   Walt Disney

MY DREAMS AND AMBITIONS

- To become a TV presenter

- To write a series of children's stories and have them made into a TV show

- To be a contestant on *Strictly Come Dancing*

- To watch a match at all 92 Football League clubs (nearly there already!)

- To present my own TV show or documentary on Asperger's and autism

THE NATIONAL AUTISTIC SOCIETY, ASPERGER SYNDROME

"People with Asperger syndrome see, hear and feel the world differently to other people. If you have Asperger syndrome, you have it for life, it is not an illness or disease and cannot be 'cured'. Often people feel that Asperger syndrome is a fundamental aspect of their identity. Autism is a spectrum condition. All autistic people share certain difficulties, but being autistic will affect them in different ways. Some people with Asperger syndrome also have mental health issues or other conditions, meaning people need different levels and types of support. People with Asperger syndrome are of average or above average intelligence. They don't have the learning disabilities that many autistic people have, but they may have specific learning difficulties. They have fewer problems with speech but may still have difficulties with understanding and processing language.

Autism, including Asperger syndrome, is much more common than most people think. There are around 700,000 autistic people in the UK – that's more than 1 in 100. People with Asperger syndrome come from all nationalities and cultural, religious and social backgrounds, although it appears to affect more men than women.

Some people with Asperger syndrome say the world feels overwhelming and this can cause them considerable anxiety. In particular, understanding and relating to other people, and taking part in everyday family, school, work and social life, can be harder. Other people appear to know, intuitively, how to communicate and interact with each other, yet can also struggle to build rapport with people with Asperger syndrome. People with Asperger syndrome may wonder why they are 'different' and feel their social differences mean people don't understand them. Autistic people, including those with Asperger syndrome, often do not 'look' disabled. Some parents of autistic children say that other people simply think their child is naughty, while adults find that they are misunderstood.

Some characteristics of Asperger's include:

Social communication

Autistic people, including those with Asperger syndrome, have difficulties with interpreting both verbal and non-verbal language like gestures or tone of voice. Many have a very literal understanding of language, and think people always mean exactly what they say. They may find it difficult to use or understand facial expressions, tone of voice, jokes and sarcasm, vagueness and abstract concepts. People with Asperger syndrome usually have good language skills, but they may still find it hard to understand the expectations of others within conversations, perhaps repeating what the other person has just said (this is called echolalia) or talking at length about their own interests. It often helps to speak in a clear, consistent way and to give people time to process what has been said to them.

Social interaction

People with Asperger syndrome often have difficulty 'reading' other people, recognising or understanding others' feelings and intentions and expressing their own emotions. This can make it very hard for them to navigate the social world. They may appear to be insensitive, seek out time alone when overloaded by other people, not seek comfort from other people, appear to behave 'strangely' or in a way thought to be socially inappropriate. They may find it hard to form friendships. Some may want to interact with other people and make friends, but may be unsure how to go about it.

Repetitive behaviour and routines

The world can seem a very unpredictable and confusing place to people with Asperger syndrome, who often prefer to have a daily routine so that they know what is going to happen every day. They may want to always travel the same way to and from school or work, or eat exactly the same food for breakfast. The use of rules can also be important. It may be difficult for someone to take a different approach to something once they have been taught the 'right' way to do it. They may not be comfortable with the idea of change, but may be able to cope better if they can prepare for changes in advance.

Highly-focused interests

Many people with Asperger syndrome have intense and highly-focused interests, often from a fairly young age. These can change over time or be lifelong, and can be anything from art or music, to trains or computers. An interest may sometimes be unusual. One person loved collecting rubbish, for example. With encouragement, the person developed an interest in recycling and the environment. Many channel their interest into studying, paid work, volunteering, or other meaningful occupations. People with Asperger syndrome often report that the pursuit of such interests is fundamental to their wellbeing and happiness.

Sensory sensitivity

People with Asperger syndrome may also experience over- or under-sensitivity to sounds, touch, tastes, smells, light, colours, temperatures or pain. For example, they may find certain background sounds, which other people ignore or block out, unbearably loud or distracting. This can cause anxiety or even physical pain. Or they may be fascinated by lights or spinning objects."

GLOSSARY OF TERMS

Autism – Autism is a lifelong, developmental disability that affects how a person communicates with and relates to other people, and how they experience the world around them. (The National Autistic Society)

ASD – Autism Spectrum Disorder. Autism is a spectrum condition. All autistic people share certain difficulties, but being autistic will affect them in different ways.

Asperger's (or Asperger syndrome or Asperger's syndrome or AS) – Asperger's is a developmental disorder characterised by significant difficulties in social interaction and nonverbal communication, along with restricted and repetitive patterns of behaviour and interests.

CAMHS – Child and Adolescent Mental Health Services. The NHS services that assess and treat young people with emotional, behavioural or mental health difficulties.

EHC or ECHP – Educational Health and Care Plan. A legal document which sets out a description of a child's needs and what needs to be done to meet those needs by education, health and social care.

LEA – Local Education Authority

LSA – Learning Support Assistant. LSAs work closely with teachers and provide support to individual pupils.

SEN – Special Educational Needs

SENCO – Special Educational Needs Co-ordinator. A SENCO is responsible for the day-to-day operation of the school's SEN policy. All mainstream schools must appoint a teacher to be their SENCO.

Statement of Special Educational Needs – a document which sets out a child's SEN and any additional help that the child should receive, now replaced by the ECHP.